The Genesis Cataclysm

The Genesis Cataclysm

Proposing a Noahic *Global* Flood within
an *Old-Earth* Scriptural Paradigm

W. JOSEPH STALLINGS

forewords by
John Marshall Crowe
and Edward N. Martin

RESOURCE *Publications* · Eugene, Oregon

THE GENESIS CATACLYSM
Proposing a Noahic Global Flood within an Old-Earth Scriptural Paradigm

Copyright © 2020 W. Joseph Stallings. All rights reserved. Except for brief quotations in critical publications or reviews, no part of this book may be reproduced in any manner without prior written permission from the publisher. Write: Permissions, Wipf and Stock Publishers, 199 W. 8th Ave., Suite 3, Eugene, OR 97401.

Unless otherwise indicated, all scripture quotations are from the Revised Standard Version (RSV) of The Holy Bible. Copyright 1946, 1952, 1971 by the Division of Christian Education of the National Council of Churches of Christ in the United States of America. All rights reserved.

Resource Publications
An Imprint of Wipf and Stock Publishers
199 W. 8th Ave., Suite 3
Eugene, OR 97401

www.wipfandstock.com

PAPERBACK ISBN: 978-1-7252-7035-0
HARDCOVER ISBN: 978-1-7252-7036-7
EBOOK ISBN: 978-1-7252-7037-4

Manufactured in the U.S.A.   08/31/20

Dedications

To Theadus, my wife,
the greatest of gifts from God and the love of my life
"He who finds a wife finds a good thing
and obtains favor from the Lord. . . . She is far more precious than jewels."
(Prov 18:22, 31:10b)

To Cassie, our daughter,
whom we love from the greatest depths of our soul,
and who serves Christ with honor

To Muffin, Charlie, Gracie, Brigat, and Rocky,
our beloved canine children,
who, as true means of divine grace, have blessed our lives far beyond human words

And, ultimately to God—Father, Son, and Holy Spirit—may you receive all the glory!

*It is the glory of God to conceal things,
but the glory of kings is to search things out.*
PROVERBS 25:2

The Bible, which has proved to be accurate wherever it can be checked out and has stood the test in little matters and in great happenings, has also told about a flood—a world-wide flood and a man along with his family who were saved from that flood because of their Ark.
DAVE BALSIGER & CHARLES E. SELLIER, JR. (1976)

Contents

Foreword by John Marshall Crowe   ix
Foreword by Edward N. Martin   xi
Introduction   xv

1 | The Issue Proper   1
2 | The Evidence of Scripture   12
3 | The Evidence of Nature   41
4 | The Evidence of Tradition   99
5 | The Final Thoughts   106

Bibliography   111

Foreword

by John Marshall Crowe

MY FIRST TWO YEARS of undergraduate work were at Presbyterian College in Clinton, SC. One day in an Old Testament Survey course, the professor and I had a disagreement. He told us that the biblical story of the Flood was not true. I immediately put up my hand. When he called on me, I commented, "Sir, Jesus Christ and the Apostle Peter speak of the Flood in the New Testament as a historical event. I would not want to call the Son of God and his Apostle Peter liars." Instead of responding directly to my comment, the professor made a sarcastic remark about his profound affinity for students "who know the Bible so well"—and then went on with class.

I wish that *The Genesis Cataclysm* had been written back then. If so, I could have presented a more complete argument. Within the bounds of Christian orthodoxy, Joe Stallings presents a systematic and thorough review of the issue. He rightly starts out with the claims of scripture, even going into the original languages, and tying it all into the final judgment upon the earth. I rejoice to see such a strong biblical stance from the start. Joe teaches that the scriptures hold the supreme place in the matter.

However, similarly to what he did in this book's antecedent, *The Genesis Column*, he also teaches that the evidence gained from looking at nature, in concurrence with the revelation of Scripture, shows the plausibility of a global Flood. Moreover, he clearly presents that this is confirmed by the ancient Flood traditions across many cultures.

Joe Stallings concludes, in agreement with his previous book, that we live on an old earth. Thus, he sees Noah's Flood as taking place before the Ice Age and, in fact, providing the conditions for its occurrence. One key point in this work is his ongoing emphasis that the Flood took place much further back in time than many others believe!

Foreword

I highly encourage you to carefully read this book. I also recommend that you do so with an apologetic mind and an evangelical spirit! If so, the message will encourage your trust in the Scriptures and build stronger still your faithful witness for God.

John Marshall Crowe, DMin
Retired Clergy
North Carolina Annual Conference
The United Methodist Church
Greenville, North Carolina

Foreword

by Edward N. Martin

IT IS WITH ANTICIPATION and great pleasure that I once again offer these preparatory remarks to one of Joe Stallings' books—this time, *The Genesis Cataclysm*. In this instance, one may note that in his previous work, *The Genesis Column* (Wipf & Stock, 2018), there is a small section of two or so pages entitled "The Timing of the Noahic Flood" found within its content (116–18). Joe has taken that small section, and expanded *it* into this current sizeable manuscript before the reader. I believe this means that, at the current rate, there are approximately fifty-five or so more books that he may (or may not) develop based on the various sections remaining in the 2018 book and this current offering. You may be hearing from me again soon!

In many ways, Joe's couple of books here in the Genesis Series cover basic human concerns, e.g., of the possible consistency and consonance of two or more ideas or concepts, paradigms, or theories; the nature, limits, strictures, and conditions of human knowledge and justified belief; and the proper alignment of oneself and one's being, in all its dimensions, with the great and bountiful gifts the Creator has bestowed so lovingly upon us. What are these gifts? Like the ancient Magi coming to adore the Christ Child (at least, according to tradition), as well as the parts of ancient Gaul, there are three.

First and foremost, there is the gift that we *are*: God has created us. Christian theologians have always held that God did not have to create at all; there was no inner necessity in the divine being that compelled God to create as he did. He would have been completely fulfilled and complete in his own blessed trinitological nature, filled and filling in paternal, filial, and pneumatic loving relationships.

Second, but even more, the fact that, in spite of our hateful rebellion against the Lord, still *he loves us*, and indeed, pours out his love to us through the bountiful life, ministry, teaching, death, resurrection and current co-ruling and co-reigning of our Lord Jesus Christ. God's love to us is not satisfied with our mere being-in-the-world; he pays us, as C. S. Lewis tells us, the "intolerable compliment" of loving us, pursuing us, causing us (if we will but agree to it and say "Yes, Father") to become more than we could ever imagine ourselves to be.

Third, along with these great, supererogatory gifts, we also have this gift: that of being made in God's image, of having the capacities of possibly loving him, along with the capacities of thinking—even pondering—wondering, imagining and conceiving, researching and discovering, philosophizing and theologizing, remembering, reasoning, believing, doubting and knowing, deliberating and choosing, introspecting, dreaming, playing, composing, writing, recounting and narrating (e.g. of history), preferring, being useful and resourceful for others, and being social and moral beings who can bring God praise, worship and adoration. In order for humans to be and to do—to participate in (a richly Platonic concept)—the full array of personhood with which God has made us, we have to have some way to be located at a somewhere and a somewhen, and to be distinguishable one person from another, yet re-identifiable as the *same* person over those somewhens. "A body he has prepared" for *us*. These embodied persons he has placed in a common, shared space, which we call our *world*. Before God could ever make us, he made the world first to provide us with a suitable environment, full of other living things, and incredibly, space and time, causality and regularity of law and action—a real world in which to live and move and have our being.

Once having created us, a part of God's package-deal is that he would reveal himself to us. For, if he loves us with an unremitting love, and *knows* that there is no other way available by which we can be happy but by the knowledge and satisfaction of knowing God, he must show himself to us. How does a spiritual being like our Father do that when we are material beings whose atmosphere is that of a planet with a real live history and dynamic past, present and future?

Into that lawlike atmosphere, God gave us a revelation of himself, and even caused these truths to be written down through his "God-breathed" manifestation of himself by forty different authors over a 2000-year period, giving us in time what we would have as the completed Holy Scriptures.

Foreword

But there is a problem: our rebellious sin has led to separation from God and to death. Who will save us from this bondage of sin and death? But thanks be to God through Jesus Christ our Lord! (Rom 7:24-25)

When one combines these above elements, one comes to understand what Joe gives us in this book: a desire that we humans have to take God's sure revelation and to *understand* it in light of our shared empirically real world. How do we *as humans* understand our present and our future, still to be revealed? The *past*. We have to look to the past to receive and appreciate God's revelation to us in the Bible.

I am very pleased to inform the reader that Joe has, as a matter of Christian conviction, made it a priority—indeed, an *apriority*—to see that God's Word comes first no matter what theories we may entertain or construct concerning models of the past. In the book before the reader, Joe makes it his *point of departure* that God's Word must determine the boundaries of any acceptable model of the Flood spoken of in Genesis 6-8. And Joe gives us a lot of cogent reasoning about why we should believe that the Bible speaks of a *universal Flood event*. Even if in the flurry of data to be considered there are some inconsistent accounts—and *there are and will be*—still, God says that the universal Flood is real, that it happened in real space-time history, that it is a part of complete Christian orthodoxy to believe this—without which other doctrines will not make complete sense.

But *when did the Flood occur*? Joe here takes these God-bestowed gifts above of reasoning, reflection, theologizing and philosophizing, and creates a paradigm for our consideration which says that Scripture must be first; and, there are some good reasons to think that the scriptural evidence for a universal Flood is plausibly consistent with what we do see in science. If all truth is God's truth, we expect and hope for a coherence, a consistency. But can we make consistent an OEC view of the days of creation—and of *a universal Flood event*? I welcome you to Joe's offering. It is a great read and great challenge that all believers need to study and consider. This book fills a niche in a unique way in the literature, and I hope the reader will strap in and appreciate the ride! Joe is to be commended for his patient and balanced treatment of a wide array of excellent sources and compelling arguments. A treat awaits you!

Edward N. Martin, PhD
Professor and Chair of Philosophy
Liberty University
Lynchburg, Virginia

Introduction

A NUMBER OF YEARS ago, when I first began the research that eventually became *The Genesis Column* origins correlation model, I had no intention of carrying out any deep exploration of the Flood of Noah. Though the event had always fascinated me and, over the years, I had read a number of books about it, including, of course, the broadly popular work by Balsiger and Sellier, *In Search of Noah's Ark* (1976),[1] it was never more than just a peripheral subject of interest. Certainly, I recognized that the Flood was an important divine action within the purview of biblical history and knew that the event would have to be addressed; yet, it wasn't until I began seeing the details of the origins correlation model fall into place that I finally concluded that, in the greater scheme of things, the Noahic Flood was *vitally* significant in its own right and had major ramifications for our understanding of the terrestrial order. Thus, a related, but separate course of research began for me.

As I read and studied further, I became aware that the current views on the Flood and the various placements of the event in time were not to me satisfactory. While being a steadfast and indefatigable advocate of Old-Earth Creationism (OEC),[2] I found myself at odds with many fellow OECs who typically held to a regional (usually Mesopotamian) Flood view. Of course,

---

1. Balsiger and Sellier, Jr., *In Search of Noah's Ark*. As a young teenager, I remember reading this book and then watching the television documentary of the same name with a bunch of my friends. We were all enthralled by the mystique and captivated by the notion that perhaps someone had actually found the Ark.

2. More specifically, Old-Earth Progressive Creationism. See *The Genesis Column*, 1–6. We believe that both the scriptural and natural revelations proclaim in unison that "These are the *generations* [Hebrew *toledot*] of the heavens and the earth when they were created" (Gen 2:4a)—viz., these are the successive and lengthy periods of creation and ongoing existence.

INTRODUCTION

my understanding also found itself automatically in contrast with the advocates of Young-Earth Creationism (YEC) because of the narrow constraints of their time-line (including that of an *extremely* recent Flood placement). Furthermore, in light of the various advocations of OEC and Theistic Evolutionism that are based on (or otherwise associated with) the recent resurgence of the Framework Hypothesis of the biblical creation narrative[3]—and with that, often a symbolic or hybridic Flood view—there were just many elemental features inherent to these formulations that, to me, did not seem weighty and persuasive. In my understanding, none of these interpretations seemed to adequately fit either a wholesome reading of the Noahic text nor God's bigger picture. With all this, I found myself being compelled to engage in a new and much different sort of exploration of the matter.

I must acknowledge that, being an investigator, my research of the subject has traversed across many variant perspectives and angles. In fact, in this text, I engage applicable scholars from some very diverse views and disciplines. The quest is accomplished simply with one goal in mind: the earnest seeking of truth.

A lot of different people—even many with greatly antithetical positions—can have much to say that adds richness to the subject at hand. Sometimes scholars can make important discoveries and wisdom-filled assertions that find their placement into our postulation in ways that would never have even remotely occurred to them; or perhaps, even in ways that they never would have intended nor desired. As I have sifted through the many works and the abundance of raw data, I have tried, with God's guidance, to consciously remain open to these kinds of possibilities. When it comes down to it, it is always about frame of reference and about the way that things—however true those things may be on their own merit alone—are seen and understood in relation to other meritorious truths. Sometimes we miss the fullness of truth because we are not looking with both eyes open. And sometimes even undisputed facts can be incorrectly placed within the structures of a paradigm—even when the wider paradigm itself is quite plausible. There is a forest. And there are trees. Both. We do our level best when we don't miss—or misappropriate—either one.

As I previously set forth in my first book, *The Genesis Column* (Wipf & Stock, 2018), it is my unwavering conviction that there exists a great divine meta-narrative of and within all created existence.[4] God is both working in

---

3. For instance, think Meredith Kline and Bruce Waltke.

4. For instance, see *The Genesis Column*, 2. In reference to Genesis 1–2, I write: "I have come to believe that those two chapters tie the whole biblical revelation together.

INTRODUCTION

and revealing himself through history. God not only created everything that is, but is decisively going somewhere with all that he has created. He is working resolutely and purposefully in and through all of the space, time, matter, and energy of which his created order consists. Yet, that creation—originally perfect—is currently fallen. Our rebellious Adamic touch has tainted and marred the Edenic Paradise and everything that is part of that order has been afflicted. Therefore, the work of God goes on through a process whereby the restoration of fallen Original Creation will surely come to pass in the ultimate culmination of final New Creation. Until that point in God's mysterious kairological time, "the creation [still] waits with eager longing for the revealing of the sons of God" when "the creation itself will [then] be set free from its bondage to decay and obtain the glorious liberty of the children of God" (Rom 8:19, 21). For now, however, we must be content to live in this still-broken age amidst the tensioned surety of the *not (quite) yet*.

As such, this process of renewal has been and remains continually painful for the totality of fallen creation. All of creation—whether organic or inorganic—truly groans, cries, struggles, and grieves in its own way as it waits for the new glory to finally appear (Rom 8:22–24). Despite the ongoing renewing work of God (see John 5:17)—indeed, in accordance with that work—the fall has its inundative consequences. Persevering through these consequences requires our trust in the Christ of our salvation and our ongoing patient endurance.

While the very notion of divine judgment is never a comfortable matter among compassionate people—and quite frankly unwelcome in many circles—it is strongly presented as a reality in the Bible. Therefore, all thoughtful seekers and followers of Christ must deal with it straight up. It cannot be avoided without negating a significant part of the scriptural revelation. According to Scripture, God has punctuated chronological history with three great purging judgments: the Fall Judgment (Gen 3), the Flood Judgment (Gen 6–8), and the Final Judgment (Rev 1–22). Within the scarlet thread that runs throughout the holy text, all three are inseparably intertwined. In the light of God's complete omniscience and perfect holiness, all three have been deemed to be necessary.

While this book focuses specifically on the reality of the Noahic Flood, it will be apparent that all three judgments are in play throughout

---

I have also come to believe that those two chapters provide a special intersection with the truth of natural revelation and present a composite picture of the whole of created reality."

INTRODUCTION

the narrative. If it wasn't for the Adamic Fall, there would be no Flood nor Eschaton. Yet, the Fall leads to the Flood, which points to the Eschaton.

Note also that this book can be read as a stand-alone entity. It is, however, highly suggested that one first read *The Genesis Column* prior to reading *The Genesis Cataclysm*. The former sets the stage for the latter; and the latter is an extension from and a derivative appendage of the former. Moreover, there are a number of concepts discussed in *The Genesis Column* (including, of course, the Inundative Corruption Hypothesis, and then perhaps most importantly, the model's overall meta-narrative presentation) of which being familiar with would be quite helpful in understanding *The Genesis Cataclysm*. The Flood fits into the total picture of God's redemptive program and serves to magnify the extreme seriousness in *chronos* by which the Almighty, in his holiness, takes our creaturely sin and rebellion. In fact, in all honesty, within the total purview of the Genesis Column Model, one cannot seriously hold to a view of anything less than a *global* Noahic Flood.

In reading this book, may our thinking be seriously provoked and may we enjoy—yet mostly, benefit—from the provocation.

W. Joseph Stallings
Wilson, North Carolina
Eastertide 2020

1

The Issue Proper

> Christian scholars have an obligation to lead the way toward a
> renewed reverence for God's truth wherever it can be found. . . .
> Christians should be preeminently motivated to investigate the
> intricacies of God's created order, confident that a better grasp of
> both God's Word and God's works will be forthcoming.[1]

Within the story of human antiquity, there are probably few things more enigmatic—and more controversial—than the matter of the Noahic Flood. As geomorphologist David R. Montgomery forthrightly states: "Noah's story is central to one of the longest-running debates between science and religion as people sought, and still seek, to reconcile scriptural interpretation with observations of the natural world."[2] In this regard, he is absolutely right on the mark. There is frequent debate among scholars, even among those who are evangelical Christians, about such things as the Flood's historicity, extensiveness, and significance. In their classic 1961 book, *The Genesis Flood*, Whitcomb and Morris make this statement:

> The question of the historicity and the character of the Genesis Flood is no mere academic issue of interest to a small handful of scientists and theologians. If a worldwide flood actually destroyed the entire antediluvian human population, as well as all land

---

1. Young, *The Biblical Flood*, 312.
2. Montgomery, *The Rocks Don't Lie*, xiv.

animals, except those preserved in a special Ark constructed by Noah (as a plain reading of the Biblical record would lead one to believe), then its historical and scientific implications are tremendous. The great Deluge and the events associated with it necessarily become profoundly important to the proper understanding of anthropology, of geology, and of all other sciences which deal with historical and prehistorical events and phenomena.[3]

Just what one believes about the Noahic Flood has tremendous implications across a vast array of scientific and historical arenas. Furthermore, from an integrationist perspective, we believe that these scientific and historical implications are all tied together by the Flood's importance within the realm of orthodox-evangelical Christian theology. As such, Whitcomb and Morris add this:

But of even greater importance are the implications of the mighty Flood of Genesis for Christian theology. For that universal catastrophe speaks plainly and eloquently concerning the sovereignty of God in the affairs of men and in the processes of nature. Furthermore, it warns prophetically of a judgment yet to come, when the sovereign God shall again intervene in terrestrial events, putting down all human sin and rebellion and bringing to final fruition His age-long plan of creation and redemption.[4]

It is our contention that the Flood must be viewed from both the broad and the narrow as well as the blatant and the hidden perspectives in order to grasp its veracity.[5] Following Whitcomb and Morris, the Scriptures do not statically present the Noahic Flood as just another notable event which happened sometime in the distant past, but as a divine apex action inundated with profound theological meaning that occurred within the bounds of both natural and human history. They also offer a reminder that the Flood event

3. Whitcomb and Morris, *The Genesis Flood*, xix.
4. Whitcomb and Morris, *The Genesis Flood*, xix.
5. The old saying about "the forest and the trees" constantly comes to mind. If we only look at the forest, we may very well miss many, if not all, of the trees. If we only look at the trees, we may not see the entire forest right before our eyes. For example, there are a number of trace evidences that could point to a global Flood, yet may not be definitive in and of themselves. However, several such evidences when viewed together may be considered to be much more convincing. Thus, an investigator would do well to look at each piece of evidence individually *and* then consider them all as a composite whole before finally reaching a conclusion. This is an important principle of good forensics and good basic investigation. Furthermore, it is also imperative to view the Flood within the greater eschatological context. God is indeed going somewhere—an ultimate destination—with his actions in and through all of those things of which he has created.

The Issue Proper

of history serves as a precursor to another cataclysmic event—an event in *chronos* that is still yet to come—the eschatological return of Christ and the Final Judgment. This particular concept, as shall be later shown, is extremely important.

There are three major views concerning the Flood. First, there is the traditional view, which posits that the Flood was an actual historical event that transpired as a global, worldwide cataclysm. Second, there is the local view, which posits that the Flood was an actual occurrence, but was limited and somewhat regional in nature (most regional models place the Flood in the Mesopotamian area). Third, there is the symbolic view, which holds that the Flood was not an actual historical event, but rather a story written to teach theological truth.[6] It should be additionally noted that it is also possible to devise creative hybrid understandings as well. For instance, some scholars will formulate various combinations of the local and the symbolic view (e.g., Longman and Walton).

We immediately refute the symbolic view on the grounds that the biblical account of the Noahic Flood is self-affirming of its historical nature. While scholars may attempt to refute the historicity of the biblical Flood on empirical and extra-biblical grounds, it is a pointless endeavor to claim that the intention of the scriptural revelation is not to present the Deluge as an actual, factual event.[7] As Richard M. Davidson[8] states:

> [W]e must note the evidences within the biblical account affirming the historical nature of the Flood. In the literary structure of the Flood story, the genealogical frame or envelope construction (Genesis 5:32 and 9:28–29) plus the secondary genealogies (Genesis 6:9–10 and 9:18–19) are indicators that the account is

---

6. Davidson, "Biblical Evidence," 79

7. It is the common praxis among those who attempt such a refutation to disregard the built-in textual intention of Scripture—even when that teaching is blatantly obvious on its face and truly leaves no other viable options—and thus, in so doing, to subordinate the Bible to accommodate their perception of nature. When it comes down to it, the underlying presumption is that nature actually carries more weight in a given discussion. As just one representative sampling of this from among many other similar works, see David R. Montgomery, *The Rocks Don't Lie* (2012). He concludes: "We may argue endlessly about how to interpret the Bible, but the rocks don't lie. They tell it like it was" (257). Of course, this view fails to seriously consider the duo-reality that, first, the natural order is fallen; and that, second, the Bible, without blemish, tells it like it was, is, and forever will be.

8. Davidson, who is Professor of Old Testament Exegesis at Andrews University, has done a tremendous amount of work concerning the biblical teachings of the Noahic Flood.

> intended to be factual history. The use of the genealogical term *toledot* ([Hebrew for] 'generations,' "account") in the Flood story (6:9) as throughout Genesis (13 times, structuring the whole book), indicates that the author intended this story to be as historically veracious as the rest of Genesis. Walter Kaiser analyzes the literary form of Genesis 1–11 and concludes that this whole section of Genesis must be taken as "historical narrative prose" . . . [Furthermore] The historical occurrence of the Flood is part of the saving/judging acts of God, and its historicity is assumed and essential to the theological arguments of later biblical writers employing Flood typology.[9]

He concludes: "Thus according to the biblical writers, far from being a non-historical, symbolical, or mythical account written only to teach theological truths, the Flood narrative is intended to accurately record a real, literal, historical event."[10] We concur with Davidson that the Noahic Flood, as recorded in Scripture, was a divine event set in human *space-time* history.

Having said that, there are those—even some who are professing evangelicals purported to have a conservative theological bent, such as Francisco—who claim that the Noahic text should not be modernly interpreted as it appears plainly written. According to this view, the narrative was simply given as somewhat of an emblematic story (probably itself derived from "correspondencies between the Hebrew and Babylonian stories" which are likely "based upon a common antecedent,"[11] whether that antecedent was an even older story or group of stories, or an actual prior local flood event or series of local events that occurred over time, or some sort of combination of the above) which the author embedded with a (hyperbolic) Hebrew extremism literary device (i.e., in this case, by crafting it into a worldwide event) to clearly make a much stronger "moral of the story" point. In this light, Francisco states just how he perceives the real truth to be:

> The biblical account does not [really] demand the interpretation that every foot of the earth be covered with water any more than the statement in Acts 2:5, that there were in Jerusalem "devout men from every nation under heaven," claims that even men from America were there! Just as Acts declares that men were there from all the civilized world, the essential claim in Genesis 6 is that the water covered all the inhabited earth.[12]

9. Davidson, "Biblical Evidence," 79–90.
10. Davidson, "Biblical Evidence," 79–90.
11. Francisco, "Genesis," 139.
12. Francisco, "Genesis," 139. This is essentially a regional Flood view—"all the

The Issue Proper

Francisco's assertion could possibly pass some degree of logical muster if it were not for, at least, one small feature in the Noahic text: that is, the important depth detail in Genesis 7:20—"the waters prevailed above the mountains covering them from fifteen cubits deep." Mind you, not fourteen nor sixteen; not ten nor twenty; not greatly nor deeply nor barely, but *fifteen*. While we concur that the Acts 2 text (which is also historical narrative prose) does indeed utilize a Hebrew extremism device in order to make an emphatic point,[13] the comparison of the two texts is not an equal one and thus essentially presents a strawman argument. It would have been much more appropriate to compare the Noahic text with, say, the passage in John 21, specifically verse 11—"So Simon Peter went aboard and hauled the net ashore, full of large fish, a hundred and fifty-three of them." Mind you, not a hundred and fifty-two nor a hundred and fifty-four; not a hundred and fifty; not just a boatload or a lot or a few, but *a hundred and fifty-three*. These seemingly inconsequential details in the story are really not so inconsequential. Completely aside from any presumed emphatic points to be made, or from any interpretation of the meanings of these passages whatsoever, both of these texts present their details with a very narrow specificity for one reason and one reason alone: because they each chronicle *exactly* what happened. Not only did Peter and his fellow fishermen catch a whole lot of fish, but they caught 153 of them (and even "large" ones, no less). Likewise, not only did the Noahic Flood cover every foot of the planet Earth including the highest peaks (which alone is self-affirming that every foot of the ground was indeed already covered), but it covered those highest peaks to a depth of 15 cubits (which is the equivalent of 22.5 feet in our modern English system of measurement). We contend that these are both cases of *precise detail* and *narrow specificity* designating *actual history*.[14]

Meanwhile, in a vein of thought similar to that of Francisco (above), yet presented in the form of a notable hybridic variation of the symbolic view, Longman and Walton agree that the Noahic text is indeed fully intended to present a worldwide Flood event. However, in their understanding, the Mosaic author was actually using rhetorical language with graphic

---

inhabited earth," in his understanding, refers only to the Mesopotamian region.

13. Francisco is likely correct implying that there were not any Native Americans present for the Acts 2 event.

14. By the way, there are several other such details in the Noahic text as well. For example, notice the specifics given as to the Ark's dimensions (Gen 6:14–16), as well as the specifics given as to the day the Flood began (Gen 7:11), etc. Accounts with explicit details, particularly those using very precise numbers, lend themselves to being a conveyance of historicity.

imagery—not because it actually happened that way—but because anything other than a dramatic universal Flood presentation would not have the necessary impact to effectively communicate the desired theological truth.[15] In this line of thinking, the historicity (or degree of historicity) of the Flood is not essentially important; it is rather the *deeper* theological message that *really* matters.[16] The reality of its actual occurrence is, at best, secondary—perhaps even irrelevant.

Of course, the problem with these sorts of postulations is that if the event portrayed is removed from (or even diminished within) history, then perhaps the theological truth can be removed (or, at least, greatly diminished) as well. In fact, John Warwick Montgomery[17] speaks forcefully of such a divorce: "History can be removed from Christian theology only by the total destruction of theology itself."[18] The vital implication is that the truth of

---

15. Longman III and Walton, *Lost World of the Flood*, 145–49. In their particular case, Longman and Walton believe that the Noahic narrative actually does have some sort of historical event behind it (possibly some sort of spectacular local event or events), but they "cannot be sure" exactly what it may have been because "we have [physical] evidence of more than one flood that would be potential candidates for the inspiration of the story" (145); yet, they are also equally convinced that "there is absolutely no [physical] evidence for a worldwide flood" (146).

16. Longman III and Walton, *Lost World of the Flood*, 92–93. Moreover, they also state earlier in the same book: "The deepest reality, that which is most true, must not be constrained by what eyewitnesses can attest or demonstrate to have 'actually happened.' The accounts in Genesis 1–11 can be affirmed as having real events as their referents, but the events themselves (yes, they happened) find their significance in the interpretation that they are given in the biblical text. That significance is not founded in their historicity but in their theology; not in what happened (or even that something did happen) but in why it happened. What was God doing? That is where the significance is to be found" (17). As Longman and Walton try to gently navigate around this matter, they seem to be claiming that the presentation of the historical referent itself (if one does even exist) may be *less true* than the "most true" theological interpretation of that referent. In other words, the implication is that there can be a significant interpretive *why* without a fully historical *what* of which to interpret, or a significant theological meaning of something with or without the actual occurrence of that something. As such, they appear to assert that, regardless as to whether or not the Noahic Flood actually happened on the Earth as it is presented in the biblical text, we do have its story in the Bible; therefore, there is great theological truth that we can and should learn from it simply because it is a story. Unfortunately, however, this makes the Noahic narrative more akin to a fairy tale with a moral attached than to a historical narrative through which God actually worked. For many of us of particularly non-Gnostic persuasion, such a viewpoint will render even the theological lessons quite hollow and without much substance.

17. Montgomery is a renowned theologian (and attorney) who specializes in Christian apologetics.

18. Montgomery, "Karl Barth and Contemporary Theology of History," 45.

both history and theology would be mutually eradicated by their severance. The occurrence of the biblical events in general history is the bedrock of their theological truth. It is our firm conviction that the Judeo-Christian reality is an actual reality because it is indeed fully set in space-time. We believe that one of the most important features of the Hebrew-Christian scriptures is that they purport to place its recorded events in some form of actual historic geochronology. This is the very reason that the Bible regularly includes—squarely in the midst of its proclaimed theological and spiritual precepts—certain personal and historical details on its sacred pages. The point of the details is to substantiate that the particular thing recorded *really happened*. The mighty acts and lessons of God and our respondent faith and life as set in actual time and place are as fleshy real as it gets. The efficacy of the faith itself—as well as the authenticity of its theological teaching—is deeply rooted in its *historical* truth.[19] The two—history and theology—are not in conflict nor disconnected from one another, but are, in fact, necessarily commensurate. In the case of the Noahic Flood, it is presented in the Bible as a purposeful divine action that occurred in the form of a specific event on Earth and at a specific time on Earth. Its factual historicity, in every possible sense of the word, is crucial to its theological and spiritual relevance. As Davidson so aptly avers:

> The Genesis Flood narrative presents profound theology. But this theology is always *rooted* in history. Any attempt to separate theology and history in the biblical narratives does so by imposing an external norm, such as Greek dualism, upon the text. Read on its own terms, the biblical narratives, including the Flood narrative, defy attempts to read them as nonhistorical theology.[20]

Still following Davidson, yet forcefully pushing a step further, we aver that the biblical narratives even defy attempts to read them as merely some form of *semi*-historical theology (viz., having some mere kernel of historical truth deeply hidden somewhere beneath the many layers of developed fable and

---

19. Note that there are certainly times when phenomenological language is used in the descriptive scriptural presentation of certain historical events (e.g., the creation narrative of Genesis 1–2). However, such use does not negate the literal historicity of those events in any way. We strongly demonstrate this notion in *The Genesis Column* (2018).

20. Davidson, "The Genesis Flood Narrative," 52. Both Barth and Bultmann incorporate a more contemporary variation of dualism in their attempts to grapple with biblical history. We will briefly discuss Barthian neo-dualism, in particular, in the next chapter.

allegory). To diminish the historicity of the Flood in any way is to also dissipate its deeper truth in every way.[21]

There are other such biblical texts as well upon which hinge major theological truth. Imagine, for instance, the illegitimacy of Christian soteriology and eschatology if the New Testament records of the incarnation, crucifixion, resurrection, and coming consummation of Christ were merely considered to be a rhetorical and figurative storyline. Think about it: What would be the ramifications if the writers of the four Gospels intended for the resurrection of Christ narrative to be some form of hyperbole? As Montgomery again presents so forthrightly:

> The New Testament most definitely presents the Christian faith as a matter of concrete, cognitive truth. Whether one looks at Christ's demands ("Believe me that I am in the Father, and the Father in me"—John 14:11) or at the explicit creedal affirmations of the apostles ("I delivered unto you first of all that which I also received, how that Christ died for our sins according to the scriptures . . . and that he rose again the third day according to the scriptures"—1 Cor. 15:3, 4), one sees that Christianity is not primarily a matter of feeling or even action, but a religion of factual belief that yields genuine religious experience and meaningful social action, only because of its objective truth.[22]

Despite the incredible theological implications conveyed in the scriptures concerning the person and work of Christ, if Jesus did not physically and bodily rise from the grave, then he is still dead—and so is all subsequent

---

21. While there are various literary genres represented in the total body of Holy Scripture, we concur with Kaiser (mentioned above, in Davidson) that the text of Genesis 1–11 (inclusive of the Noahic text of Genesis 6–9) is intended to be a form of *historical narrative prose* (for further on this, see Kaiser, "The Literary Form of Genesis 1–11," 48–65). This means that it is to be understood similarly, not only to the other historical OT texts, but also to the NT events of Jesus's life as documented in the Gospels as well as to the events of the early apostolic church as recorded in the Acts of the Apostles. For instance, it might be duly noted that most of the tangible artifacts, etc. inherent to the human life of Christ as Jesus of Nazareth are now removed from our empirical experience or hidden from our view. This in no way negates the absolute requirement of the faith for God Incarnate to have actually lived, died, and risen in true and literal physical human form. In fact, for many, this is the basal motivation for the classic search for the historical Jesus, which continues from generation to generation. If God did not actually become physically incarnate in the human person of Jesus of Nazareth, then the Jesus Christ of Scripture and all things attributed to him in the scriptures are completely irrelevant. This is likewise certainly true with the Flood of Noah.

22. Montgomery, *Faith Founded on Fact*, 29.

The Issue Proper

Christian theology and faith.[23] No mere resurrection of Christ in the "hearts" of the people, nor some sort of mystical resurrection "within the 'kerygma'" will do it; if God-the-Son did not become physically incarnate in the human being known as Jesus of Nazareth and did not die on the Cross of Calvary (located at a specific geographic site just outside the walls of Jerusalem) and literally rise from the dead (in every physical and bodily sense), then there is no salvation available. Moreover, if that were to be the case, then all of Judeo-Christianity is a lie and the entirety of Christian faith is a farce (1 Cor 15:12–28). The unbridled telos of such thinking is essentially an insidious and hollow existentialism which conflicts with virtually every biblical tenet of evangelical-sacramental Christianity. The fact of physical and material incarnationality is the essence of the scriptural Judeo-Christian reality.[24]

So—within the realm of the empirical universe, which notion is more difficult to embrace: that God, in accordance with the OT Scriptures, caused a global Flood upon the Earth during the time of Noah; or that God, in accordance with the NT Scriptures, caused the Resurrection of Jesus from the dead during the governorship of Pontius Pilate? Which, if either, fits more securely within the parameters of common reason, everyday experience, and the evidences of naturalistic science? Certainly, the notion of God raising the dead back to life should confound the rationalistic thinker at least as much as the notion of God causing an Earth-immersive Flood.[25] Yet, again, the Scriptures equally proclaim both to be actual occurrences in the material world of which we now live. Both are proclaimed to be unqualified truth.

---

23. And, by the way, if that be the case, so are we (1 Cor 15:12–28).

24. God has willfully provided for his Kingdom actions to be accomplished within the unrestrained purview of space-time history. It has always been his ongoing plan and practice not to keep either himself or his works at a place of distance from his creatures (nor even from the enemy). Thus, he knows that, in so doing, both himself and his works will certainly be attacked and even exposed to the risk of discreditation; yet God, who is himself Truth, is willing and able to do this because he also knows that he and all of his works are completely and perfectly trustworthy and true and will ultimately be borne out as such in the plain sight of all the universe.

25. By the way, there are other resurrection events directly related to Jesus. Before Jesus died and was raised from the dead, the scriptures proclaim that Jesus himself raised, at least, three other deceased people: the son of the widow of Nain (Luke 7:11–17), Jairus' daughter (Matt 9:18–26; Mark 5:21–43; Luke 8:40–56), and Lazarus (John 11:1–44). It is upon physical resurrection which hinges *everything* about the authenticity of the Christian faith; yet, we cannot help but wonder just how truly and evidentially believable any of this can be to the global Flood disavowist? Afterall, apart from the record of Scripture and the ongoing testimony of the Church, what definitive empirical evidence is there in the natural world for any of these resurrections *by* Christ—or even for the resurrection *of* Christ?

The Genesis Cataclysm

Please know this: Neither a symbolic Christ Event—nor a symbolic Flood Event—would have any truth significance whatsoever. Taken as merely stories outside of concrete history—regardless of any lessons we try to assign to them, they both become only tall tales rendering even the lessons invalid. The doctrines and the theology of the faith must always be founded on firm and objective historical factuality.[26] Otherwise, they too—like the message-conveying fabulistic stories themselves—would be veraciously null and void. Symbolism without factuality is fluff. Therefore, with the symbolic interpretation cast aside, the issue then becomes a matter of determining whether the Flood is best understood as a global or a local/regional phenomenon.

The nature and importance of the *historic* Noahic Flood should cause those with a concern for Christian apologetics to seriously consider that the event must have indeed left its recorded footprint, both textually and terrestrially. Much chronological time has passed since the Noahic Flood event within the context of all biblical paradigms (i.e., Young-Earth = c. 4–4.5 ka[27]; Old-Earth = possibly *much* further back in time[28]), thus the overtness of the geo-terrestrial footprint has most certainly faded to some degree over the ages through natural attrition. Yet, while we resolutely and unwaveringly stand on the evidence of God's preserved scriptural revelation of the event, we are also quite confident that God has preserved at least some of the diluvial evidence in nature and history and allows it to be made presently visible to those seekers who truly want to see.[29] An inquiry into this collaborative

---

26. Note that Jesus also spoke quite "a-matter-of-factly" about the historical Noah himself and the Flood in the parallel texts of Matthew 24:37–39 and Luke 17:27 in terms of both its sure historical occurrence and its connection to a certain just-as-sure future occurrence.

27. Osgood, "The Date of Noah's Flood," 10–13. See also Sarfati, *Refuting Compromise*, 241.

28. As an OEC, Ross, for instance, seems to support a Flood timing of about 20,000 to 30,000 years ago. See Ross, *A Matter of Days*, 223. His calculation is based on a combination of certain specific historical markers (such as a relative dating for Abraham at about four thousand years ago and the interpretation of the Peleg text of Genesis 10:25 to refer to the breaking up of the Bering Strait land bridge at about 11,000 years ago) and the assumption that the life spans recorded in the genealogies of Genesis 5 and 11 are proportional to the actual passage of time. As shall be shown later, we advocate for a Flood time even much further back in time than does Ross.

29. Ross possibly disputes this. See Ross, *The Genesis Question*, 159–60. Here he states: "The assumption that clear evidence 'should' remain must be challenged. The Flood, though massive, lasted but one year and ten days. A flood of such brief duration typically does not leave a deposit substantial enough to be positively identified thousands of years later. . . . a one-year Flood in the region of Mesopotamia, even to a depth of two or three hundred feet, may leave behind insufficient evidence for a positive geological identification

The Issue Proper

(scriptural/natural/historical) assertion shall be the major quest of this book. Are there sufficient evidences to plausibly warrant positing a *global* Noahic Flood within the auspices of a specific *Old-Earth* biblical paradigm? If so, what are they?

---

ten to forty thousand years later." First, keep in mind that Ross's skepticism is grounded in a regional Flood view rather than in a global Flood view, which we refute. Second, in partial agreement with Ross, there is no doubt that there are some geological evidences—particularly depositional—which were either never substantial enough nor made permanent enough to clearly identify today as being Noahic. This will be discussed later.

2

The Evidence of Scripture

> But as for you, continue in what you have learned and have firmly believed, knowing from whom you learned it and how from childhood you have been acquainted with the sacred writings which are able to instruct you for salvation through faith in Christ Jesus. All scripture is inspired by God and profitable for teaching, for reproof, for correction, and for training in righteousness, that the man of God may be complete, equipped for every good work.[1]

We appropriately begin with the biblical revelation. The Bible—both through its Old and New Testament disclosure—is the particular written message of God revealing himself through history, especially as unveiled through his great works of "salvation through faith in Christ Jesus" (2 Tim 3:15). In light of this, the Flood narrative as found in scripture, which chronicles one of God's most awesome (and terrible) salvific works,[2] is every bit as important a cog in the historical panorama of salvation in Christ as is the creation, the fall, the passion/resurrection event, and the eschaton. The Bible is the only account of reality that reveals the entire uncorrupted framework of the greater action and movement of God. Thus, when seeking to ascertain the

---

1. 2 Tim 3:14–17.
2. Not unlike that of another coming day (see Joel 2:31–32; cf. Acts 2:19–21).

reality of the Flood, it is very important to always give *a priori* status to the biblical record.³ As Barrick emphasizes so strongly:

> All study of the Flood needs to begin with the biblical record itself. Careful analysis of the record in Genesis 6–8 should be the only basis upon which anyone considers potential geologic implications. However, in spite of the revelatory nature of the biblical record, many evangelical scholars continue to give up valuable ground to secular scientists and humanistic theories in evangelical waters without realizing that those theories and their methodologies have never been converted. While there are valuable kernels of truth buried within contemporary critical and so-called "scientific" studies, evangelicals must take great care to irradiate the material with the Word of God so as not to unknowingly and unintentionally introduce secularized thinking into the Church.⁴

Barrick's concern that evangelical Christians may inadvertently fall prey to compromise and "unknowingly and unintentionally introduce secularized thinking into the Church" is most certainly commendable; we indeed share that ideal. However, we again come to the *truth is truth* reality. While we absolutely concur with Barrick's emphasis that the biblical record should be kept in the *a priori* (and primary) position, we must be sure not to allow ourselves to become wary of taking a full-bodied integrationist approach to truth. Hanna provides some helpful thoughts:

> Authentic theology recognizes the divine and human dimensions of, and the hierarchy among, God's revelations. The divine/human incarnation of Jesus is the supreme revelation. The divine/human inspiration of Scripture is a special revelation. Nature, including

---

3. Paul asserts (above, in 2 Tim 3:14–17) that "all scripture is inspired by God," and then, as an outcome of such a divine origin, he proclaims that "the sacred writings" are definitively beneficial for the instruction (Greek *didaskalia*, lit., to instruct, teach) of Kingdom truth, for the rebuke (Greek *elegmos*, lit., to chasten, censure) of that which is contrary to Kingdom truth, and for the refinement (Greek *epanorthosis*, lit., to correct, revise) of Kingdom understandings, as well as for purposeful guidance (Greek *paideia*, lit., to perfect, make excellent) in becoming a Christian disciple and in mastering the measured ways of faithfully following Christ. As we seek to understand the universe and to take dominion over the created order—of which God has made humanity the Crown—the ultimate goal is always for our salvation and for the correspondent ongoing development of our Christian discipleship, which is always grounded in the truth of God's composite reality. This, of course, includes the revealed truth of God-events set within the bounds of space-time—the Noahic Flood being one such significant occurrence.

4. Barrick, "Noah's Flood and its Geological Implications," 252.

human nature, is a general revelation. . . . We do not undermine
God's revelation when we interpret Jesus, Scripture, and nature in
the light of each other. To do otherwise is to reject the plain teaching of Scripture itself.[5]

In essence, integrationism does not have to mean the compromise of truth; it is certainly *not* accommodationism. In fact, to the contrary, integrationism is actually the most authentic quest for the greatest and most comprehensive understanding of truth. From the Christian perspective, there is truth that can and *should* be found within all venues, even those which are deemed to be secular. The key is to capture that which is truth from whatever source it can be found (whether secular or sacred, theology or science, etc.) and then to place it (integrate it) appropriately and plausibly within the framework of a scriptural paradigm (i.e., to apply Barrick's own words above, to "take care to irradiate the material with the Word of God"). The first step to making this happen indeed does come from giving the biblical revelation the *a priori* position. For the Christian researcher, the Scriptures are both the starting point and the major source of evidence for authenticating and comprehending the Flood. This notion should even be considered to be largely suppositional and self-evident. The Scriptures are, in fact, considered to be the divine canon of God's church. Hence, as Christians and thereby members of the Body of Christ, these sacred writings should be fully treated as such. Thus, before we begin to study what the Bible has to say about the Noahic Flood itself, we will briefly and logistically speak to the matter of why the scriptures have the very *highest* place in this discussion.

THE PRIMACY OF SCRIPTURE CONCERNING THE TRUTH OF THE NOAHIC FLOOD

It should be clearly understood that, for the Christian, the Bible is far more than just another book of religious dogma. It is a divine statement of reality. It is the systematic framework and standard by which we must understand *all* of reality. As such, by its very nature, Scripture serves as an intersective and unitive point between perceived realms of truth: the mind of God and the mind of humanity, the spiritual and the physical, the supernatural order and the natural order, the sacred and the secular, etc.[6] While, for instance,

---

5. Hanna, "Science and Theology," 191. While it is true that Jesus and the Bible are not the same, please keep in mind that our greatest understanding of the ways and works of God-in-Christ are found in the scriptural revelation.

6. Like Holy Communion (Word of God through bread and wine), the Holy

The Evidence of Scripture

the *historie* and the *heilsgeschichte* (to borrow a bit of Barthian imagery) can sometimes—with great effort—be superficially parsed out into neat dialectical categories,[7] the scriptural text does not readily provide for such a convenience. By God's willful design, the *heilsgeschichte* (faith/theological history) is incarnationally embedded within and throughout the *historie* (natural/human history). The truth of the divine reality (which is reality itself[8]) is one. In addition to the supreme example of God-in-Christ Incarnate, other examples also proliferate the scriptures. We are presented in the Bible with the mind of God and are called to have the very same mind (e.g., 1 Cor 2:15–16; Phil 2:5–8); as such, we are also proffered the definitive sacramental grace conduit bridging the spiritual with and through the physical (e.g., John 6:48–51, 52–58; 1 Cor 10:16–17, 11:23–26; cf. Jas 5:13–16); and surely all of the healing miracles performed during the public ministry of Jesus indicate in the highest possible magnitude the divine tethering of the supernatural power of heaven with this fallen natural creation (e.g., the many incidents as recorded in all four Gospels).

The above categories are actually inundatively blended and conjunctive and cannot be divided—though we keep trying to do so—without causing damage to the parts or to the entirety. As Webber so vigorously avers: "[R]eason and science in the modern world, which originally developed among Christians, eventually became the enemy of God's narrative by separating the secular from the sacred and thereby opening the possibility for new gods to narrate the world."[9] In contrast, the pure biblical faith—centered in God himself becoming his creation in the form of the historical flesh and blood human, Jesus of Nazareth—will not allow for such a neat division. Truly, this most basal concept of divine incarnation (the eternal Word-made-flesh) completely demolishes such an idea. Unlike with other

---

Scriptures (Word of God through ink and paper) are a sacramental, connective conduit between the perfect God and the fallen creation.

7. See Montgomery, *Faith Founded on Fact*, 30–32. Here he briefly describes the Barthian (neo-dualism) and the Bultmanian (demythologization) efforts to create dialectical divisions of reality. Please be aware that the systems of both Barth and Bultmann were not in any way intended to be decimations of the Gospel, but were actually genuine attempts to protect and to strengthen the Christian faith from empirical attack. The problem arises, however, in their methodology as they largely remove the faith from the empirical-historical realm, and in so doing, separate it from what is reachable and real. Metaphorically speaking, this method is somewhat akin to cutting the heart out of a person in order to protect them from contracting heart disease. The intention may be good, but the person still dies.

8. God is I AM (Exod 3:14).

9. Webber, *Who gets to Narrate the World?*, 74.

world religions, Judeo-Christianity is founded not merely on some amorphous and ethereal spirituality, but upon divinely-incarnational and objective factuality.[10] From the divine perspective, there is no Barthian dualism,[11] but just one *whole* truth reality. The implications of this are considerable and are profoundly embodied in the scriptures of the Old and New Testaments.

We must not forget that at the most elemental level, along with the geological record and the rest of the natural order, the Bible is (also) a form of *physical evidence*—although non-Christian and other researchers often disregard this realism in their work. The inference is that, regardless of any spiritual and supernatural implications to be considered (and there are many), the Bible has strong elements of both historicism and empiricism in its constitution (i.e., it is an ancient message and record [historicism] transmitted in a material book form [empiricism]).[12] This is precisely by the design of God. Forensically speaking, the Scriptures are to be considered as much a piece of physical evidence as any rock, fossil, or sequence of strata. It would be an act of scholarly irresponsibility to simply dismiss the Bible as an irrelevant religious relic. This means that all competent researchers, even those who are of a more intentionally secularistic (or even a full-blown atheistic) bent, should be willing to give the Judeo-Christian Scriptures fair evidentiary consideration in order to maintain integrity in their postulations and to be resistant to reaching potentially flawed conclusions.[13] In other

---

10. Montgomery, *Faith Founded on Fact*, 29–30.

11. Montgomery, "Karl Barth and Contemporary Theology of History," 43–45. Commenting on Barth's understanding, he avers: "A dualism between earth and heaven—between history and theology—between Jesus and the Christ—between the Bible and Revelation—becomes essential; and with it, inevitably, comes a denial of Incarnation, the Word actually made flesh" (44).

12. See Martin, "Empiricism," 233. He comments, "The process of God getting his propositional revelation [i.e., the Scriptures] to us is largely empirical (transmission of the text, the act of reading)." In other words, the primary way that God provides us with his revelation is through a tangible, material, actual form. For instance, a scroll or a book fits this category.

13. Just to provide some clarification as to our primary textual approach, we practice the grammatico-historical method rather than the historical-critical method. This simply means that, rather than going heavily "behind the text" (to its prior pre-scriptural existence)—as is the case with the higher critical approach, we come to the received text *as is* and immediately treat it in its current form as *holy* scripture and the closed *canon* of the church. As critical evangelicals, this means that we utilize the lower critical (textual/contextual) approach. We certainly do recognize the contributions that higher criticism has and will continue to make to biblical study and, as such, we celebrate. Yet, our emphasis will always operate with the understanding that the scriptures on their face are first and foremost, *divine revelation*.

words, if a researcher is willing to include the evidence of nature in their quest for truth, they should also be willing to include the evidence of Holy Scripture—even if only on natural grounds—because *each* is considered to be a form of testable *empirical* evidence.

Even so, for those of us who are Christians with a very high view of both Scripture and the fullness of divine reality, affirming the biblical text as merely simple physical evidence (i.e., considering only its historical and empirical implications) is the absolute bare minimum; we know that there is also much more to it (i.e., considering also its additional vast spiritual and supernatural implications). The Bible (the eternal Word-made-text) is itself incarnational. In effect, within Christian orthodoxy, the Scriptures are understood to be divinely-revealed supernatural reality encapsulated and presented to us within a mundane natural package.

Case in point: God is the creator of nature; God is the giver of Scripture; God is the truth. In principle, there should be and is a comprehensive cohesion of reality—for God is one and cannot be self-contradictory. Nevertheless, consequential to Genesis 3, we now live in a degraded and disordered natural world where imperfection and noetic limitation abound. Therefore, from an evangelical Christian perspective of research, the Bible—not nature—must always be considered as the *primary* form of evidence (first-line evidence).[14] Both Scripture and nature are indeed divine revelation. However, the current version of nature exists in a fallen state.[15] It still bears a semblance of its former pre-fallen self,[16] yet—like it's co-fallen Adamic divinely-ordained caretaker (humanity)[17]—it is nonetheless corrupted and grossly marred. Meanwhile, Scripture, while given to us in the divinely preserved form of an accessible "jar of clay" (i.e., a human book), does not exist in a fallen state. It is the Word

---

14. In our current dispensation, natural revelation is *always* second-line evidence.

15. For further on the effects of the Adamic fall on nature, see the chapter, "The Matter of Corruption," in *The Genesis Column*, 7–32.

16. Yes, even in fallenness, nature does still declare the glory of God (see Ps 19:1; cf. Rom 1:19–25), but there must be the scriptural Word of God to make complete the message and the meaning. (The natural order is neither independent, self-sustaining, nor extremely *particular* in its divine revelation.) In the coming New Creation, the two "Books" of God—the truth of Scripture and the truth of nature—will blend into a perfect coherence of reality; until then, however, the Scriptures remain the ultimate record of truth to which we must cling. That is precisely why they were given to us by God: to provide us with a supernatural light as we navigate our darkened natural path.

17. Despite the Adamic fall, we still bear the image of God. It is broken, but not destroyed. Praise be to the Almighty! God-in-Christ is even now in the process of repairing the damage and will ultimately complete it in perfection (Phil 1:6).

The Genesis Cataclysm

of God-in-text,[18] and thus—like God-in-Christ Incarnate (Jesus), who is the Word of God-in-flesh[19]—by its supernatural theo-*logos* nature,[20] remains impervious to the effects of the Adamic fall.[21] By the blueprint of the Almighty, both in the person of Jesus of Nazareth and in the presentation of the Holy Scriptures, the perfect Word of God has been incarnationally and purposefully implanted within the midst of a concrete and very tangible fallen reality—even becoming as one with creation (divine *logos*-in-flesh = Jesus; divine *logos*-in-text = Scripture), while itself yet still remaining untainted by the pervasive fallenness.[22] This alone gives Scripture first-line evidential privilege.[23]

In our current fallen reality, Scripture and nature are not on an equal par. Despite having the same author, nature—as it exists now—pales in comparison with Scripture concerning stand-alone veridical value. Therefore, all of natural revelation (second-line evidence) must be viewed through the lens of Scripture (first-line evidence) and not the reverse. At any and all points of authentic friction, Scripture—not nature—must necessarily always carry the day. It is at these friction points that our interpretation of nature must be either rejected outright or revised to become confluent as much as

---

18. 2 Tim 4:2; Heb 4:12.

19. John 1:1, 14.

20. See Mounce, "logos," in *Complete Expository Dictionary*, 803. Here we refer to the "logos of God" (i.e., the authoritative communication by God of his truth) as divinely manifested in Christ himself and his teaching, as well as in the scriptural canon of his Church.

21. Since God is untainted, the Word of God cannot be tainted; 2 Tim 3:16 ("inspired" = Greek *theopneustos*, lit., "God breathed out"); also, see Wesley, "Witness of Our Own Spirit," 1:302–3.

22. At the Cross of Calvary, Jesus of Nazareth, born of God the Holy Spirit *and* the human Mary—thus being himself the incarnate Word of God (John 1) who had become one with his creation through his becoming fully human while remaining fully God, yet without having any sin and fallenness of his own, subsumed the guilt of all sin and its corollary effects of fallenness and then died with them—effectually reversing Genesis 3 and consigning sin and fallenness to its own death (2 Cor 5:21; 1 Pet 2:24). Subsequently, with his Resurrection, he then instigated the great primordial sign-act of *new creation* (fulfilling Matt 12:39–40: "the sign of the prophet Jonah"), which is yet awaiting its full and final manifestation at the eschaton (Matt 19:28—Jesus refers to this with the Greek *palingenesia*, "new genesis"). God entered and essentially became his creation with the purpose of its guaranteed ultimate redemption and complete renewal. (Relatedly, note that the Sacrament of Holy Communion—given to us by Christ himself on the Friday immediately before his Resurrection—is the ongoing sign-act of the *new covenant*.)

23. It also shows how God chooses to work most powerfully and incarnationally through the ordinary and natural things that he has made. This is the definitive sacramentality of God.

possible with our *responsible* interpretation of the plain and intended message of the biblical text.[24]

Without the powerful magnification of the biblical revelation, nature alone—in its fallenness, makes no complete sense and has no final meaning. Without the scriptural meta-narrative providing the framework of reality and the divine direction of ultimate destiny, the fallen natural order itself has no purpose and provides a grossly inaccurate and incomplete presentation of existence.[25] Yet, when subordinated to the purview of the Bible and seen in the light of its grand scheme, the evidences of the natural order—though fallen—can be understood to fluidly integrate into their proper place and provide additional truth detail. God—through his indwelling Holy Spirit—can enable us to see just enough of the connections (even through the murkiness of this corrupted universe) to become assured of the deeper cohesion of divine truth and reality.[26] As Edward N. Martin asserts: "Even if we look at human epistemology naturalistically . . . it is reasonable to believe that experience is a reliable and justified source of knowledge only if it flowers within a [Judeo-Christian] supernaturalistic metaphysics."[27] Remembering this precept is especially important when studying the issue of the Noahic Flood since many authorities deny the historicity of the Deluge (particularly a global version) on various natural-empirical grounds. (The evidence of nature will be discussed in the next chapter.)

---

24. See Payne, "Foreward," in *The Genesis Column*, xiv. He states succinctly: "Ultimately, we affirm that [biblical] revelation declares truth, and that science attempts to discover truth. To the extent that science discovers truth, that truth must align with revelation when revelation is properly understood and applied." NOTE: For some helpful resources on responsible biblical interpretation, please see the following suggested books: *Wesley, Wesleyans, and Reading Bible as Scripture* (Green and Watson, eds.); *Practicing Theological Interpretation* and *Seized by Truth* (Green); and *The Art of Reading Scripture* (Davis and Hays, eds.). These works present highly-textured perspectives on the subject of hermeneutics and are all quite thoughtful and well worth the read.

25. For an excellent sense of this meta-narrative concept, please read Wesley's sermon, "The General Deliverance," 2:437–50.

26. Certainly, on this side of the New Kingdom, while our learning continues and our knowledge base expands, we will never come to know the greater portion of the minutiae as to how this reality all fits together (1 Cor 13:9–12). There is a grand mystery to existence. Yet, in the meantime, God does give us the opportunity to seek and to find what we need in order to be faithful to his loving salvific purposes (Matt 7:7–8). As Hanna reminds us: "God does not promise to remove every doubt, but He gives sufficient evidence as a basis for faith. The Bible strengthens the intellect and is the norming source and standard for the reasons for our faith in Jesus" ("Science and Theology," 190).

27. Martin, "Empiricism," 233.

The Bible itself stands as *the* towering material record and divinely-given supernaturalistic witness of the Flood's occurrence. It is from this very perspective of scriptural primacy that the Noahic Flood will now be addressed. What does the biblical text present on its face about the Flood? This will be discussed from the variant textual angles of the Flood's scope, unique difference, universal emphasis, theological context, and view within the realm of the New Testament writings.

THE TEXTUAL PRESENTATION CONCERNING THE SCOPE OF THE NOAHIC FLOOD

There are two key Hebrew words found throughout the Genesis Flood text—Hebrew *erets* (whole earth [planet], land, ground, countries[28]) and Hebrew *adamah* (ground, piece of ground, earth as material substance, ground as earth's visible surface, land, territory, country[29])—that directly relate to the Flood's physical extensiveness (i.e., how wide did the Flood extend?). There are also two key Hebrew words in the text—Hebrew *har* (mountain [esp., mountains of high elevation], hill, hill-country, mountain-region[30]) and Hebrew *gaboahh* (high, lofty, tall, elevated, exalted, haughty, loftiness[31])—that directly relate to its physical depth (i.e., how deep were the waters of the Flood?). Just how one contextually interprets these words is of foundational importance in determining how one understands the biblical revelation of the Noahic Flood.

The Hebrew *erets*

A survey of the Genesis 6–8 text shows that Hebrew *erets* is used thirty-seven times (Gen 6:4, 5, 6, 11 [x2], 12 [x2], 13 [x2], 17 [x2]; 7:3, 4, 6, 10, 12, 14, 17 [x2], 18, 19, 21 [x2], 23, 24; 8:1, 3, 7, 9, 11, 13, 14, 17 [x3], 19, 22) and Hebrew *adamah* is used eight times (Gen 6:7, 20; 7:4, 8, 23; 8:8, 13, 21). Comparatively, this means that *erets* has nearly a five to one numerical superordination to *adamah* in the text giving it great emphatic superiority. It also means that it is highly probable that the author was being very intentional in giving *erets* the majority usage. Though *erets* and *adamah* can

---

28. Brown et al., *Hebrew Lexicon*, 75–76 (H776).
29. Brown et al., *Hebrew Lexicon*, 9–10 (H127).
30. Brown et al., *Hebrew Lexicon*, 249–50 (H2022).
31. Brown et al., *Hebrew Lexicon*, 147 (H1364).

both carry the local meaning of "ground" or "land," we contend that the somewhat alternate use of both words in the narrative was not merely a random semantic interchange. In fact, we suggest that the usage was intended to show a clear differentiation contextually between the Earth as a planet (*erets*) and the inhabitable land upon the Earth (*adamah*).[32] It should be additionally noted that, of the two words, only *erets* can effectively carry the global meaning of "whole earth" (as in the sense of *planet*),[33] although *adamah* can carry the non-local meaning of all the *land* or *ground* on the face of the Earth.

It has been commonly argued that another word, Hebrew *tebel* (world[34]), would have been a better choice for the Mosaic author if he had intended to convey a planetary or global scope for the Flood.[35] This particular argument from silence is extremely weak and does not hold much substance. The word *tebel* is not only absent from the Flood narrative, but also from the entire *creation* narrative (e.g., Gen 1:1—"heavens and the earth": Hebrew *shamayim eth erets*; note the use of *erets*, which is intended to imply an "all things" totality).[36] Furthermore, *tebel* is never used in the entire Pentateuch and never used in any narrative section of the Old Testament. Of its thirty-nine usages in the Hebrew Bible, all are found in poetic texts and most are used as a parallelism and as a poetic synonym with *erets* (not *adamah*).[37] Therefore, we conclude that the primary contextual usage of *tebel* (i.e., as a parallelism and synonym with *erets*; viz., *tebel* = *erets*) in the poetic portion of the Scriptures actually provides *reinforcement* to the global interpretation of *erets* in the Noahic narrative text.

There are scholars, such as Ross and Hill, who argue that Hebrew *erets* should not be interpreted in the Genesis text as referring to the planet Earth because Mosaic society had not yet developed a truly global conception of the world.[38] In fact, Ross states:

---

32. Note that this is contrary to the sole use of Hebrew *yom* for "day" in Genesis 1–2.

33. Strong, *Hebrew and Aramaic Dictionary*, 1, 14. Compare *adamah* (H127) and *erets* (H776). Strong asserts that *erets* can mean "the earth at large."

34. Brown et al., *Hebrew Lexicon*, 385 (H8398).

35. For example, see Archer, Jr., *A Survey of Old Testament Introduction*, 194. Also, see Enns, "How should we interpret the Genesis flood account?."

36. Compare Greek *pas ktisis*, i.e., "whole creation" (e.g., Rom 8:22). For more on this concept of totality, see Stallings, "The Meaning of 'Whole Creation,'" in *The Genesis Column*, 23–29. Also, see Hasel's footnote below.

37. Davidson, "Biblical Evidence," 81.

38. Ross, *The Genesis Question*, 146–47. Also, see Hill, "The Noachian Flood," 181.

> Our global perspective naturally colors our interpretation of Scripture. When we encounter such phrases in Genesis 7 as "under the entire heavens" and "every living thing on the face of the earth [*erets*]," we see that face under the heavens as a sphere, a planet. However, in every one of the world's languages such expressions must always be understood in their reasonable context. What constitutes "the entire heavens" and "the face of the earth [*erets*]" in the perspective of ancient peoples? We must interpret in light of their frame of reference, not ours.[39]

Ross is absolutely correct in emphasizing the need for interpretative contextuality. This is a basic principle of sound hermeneutics. A text cannot mean what it was never intended to mean. However, there are two important realities to seriously consider in this matter.

First, as mentioned above, it is not plausible to think that the Mosaic intention of scriptural phrases such as *shamayim eth erets* was not meant to refer to *all things*—even if the common Mosaic understanding of what those phrases entailed was limited.[40] Thus, in the creation context, the use of *erets* (or *tebel*, if that word had been used) would certainly mean the Earth in its entirety, regardless of whether the common terrestrial view of the day concerning such entirety was that of some large territory as far as the eye could see, a large sphere, a flat projection with four corners, or some other phenomenological conceptualization involving pillars and firmament.

Second, and far more importantly, whose frame of reference—the mortal human author/actor or the eternal divine Author/Actor—should be primarily contemplated concerning the intended meaning of a biblical narrative (i.e., that presumed to be divine *revelation*), particularly one with natural history implications (where no human being could be a competent observer or, alas, an observer at all)? Indeed, both should be duly considered. However, the ultimate omniscient Author of the inspired text (God) is always well aware of the greater global and cosmic reality—i.e., God is the

---

39. Ross, *The Genesis Question*, 146.

40. See Kaiser, "The Literary Form of Genesis 1–11," 48. Here he states: "The primary task of the Biblical scholar is to unfold the meaning of the text of Scripture as it was originally intended to be understood by the writer of that text. Those ideas, meanings, and truth-intentions which he had in mind are the first order of business. Further, if the concept of Biblical authority is to be introduced into the discussion, it will only heighten rather than decrease the intensity of the search to get back to that original writer's thought; for he is the man who claims to have heard the revelation of God." So, in light of Kaiser, the question is this: What did the Mosaic author, while receiving this sweeping and all-embracing creation revelation from God and writing it down, actually believe about the extent of the Noahic Flood?

The Evidence of Scripture

Creator and Sustainer of all things. While Moses and his contemporaries may or may not have viewed geography (and cosmology) as expansively as we do today (and while they may have been led to describe their understanding of the natural order somewhat phenomenologically—which, by the way, we still often do today: e.g., the sun "rises" and "sets," etc.), the message and efficacy of the Genesis text is not ultimately limited by any narrowness in human understanding at any given point in time (despite the perspective of the original human writer).

Moreover, there always remains the possibility of additional and expanded *illumination* to later generations of Christian researchers through the guidance of the Holy Spirit. This can occur through the continued study of both theology and natural science and should be expected. After all, such study is part of the divine dominion mandate given to humanity. Of course, future illumination does not negate in any way the fullness of meaning inherent to the biblical revelation from its very inception. That fullness of divine truth was always in the text, even if and when humanity did not see it nor completely understand it.[41]

This concept can and should be applied to the Noahic text by not disregarding the global interpretation of *erets* concerning the scope of the Flood. We believe that the Mosaic author, who was not physically present at the time of the Flood, reasonably may have understood the event to have been worldwide (regardless of whatever world image may or may not have been in his mind at that moment) as he recorded it under divine inspiration. The image that is textually presented is completely expansive. It is quite interesting that Bernhard W. Anderson, an esteemed Old Testament scholar who was of the higher critical school, made the following assertion as to the meaning of the Mosaic text of Genesis 7:11–24: "Here the flood was not caused by a rain storm but was a cosmic catastrophe resulting from opening the *windows of the heavens* (or the firmament) and the upsurging of the *fountains of the great deep* (or the subterranean chaos; cf., 1:6–8). Thus the earth was threatened with a return to pre-creation chaos (1:2)."[42] Hence, according to Anderson,

---

41. While the personal understandings of the Mosaic author were likely not as scientific as ours are today, the fact that the Genesis writings themselves are divine revelation carries their innate truth beyond Moses to us and even beyond us to the indefinite future. For example, see these various *cosmic inference* OT texts, all of which transcend any specific chronological time and are completely valid for all such time: Job 9:8; Ps 104:2; Isa 40:22; 42:5; 44:24; 45:12; 48:13; 51:13; Jer 10:12; 51:15; Zech 12:1. Indeed, each of them utilize phenomenological imagery, yet the potential modern implications for science are infinite.

42. Anderson, "Genesis annotations," 9 (italics his); cf. *Understanding the Old Testament*, 459. See also, Davidson, "The Genesis Flood Narrative," 75: "Humankind's marring

the message of the Mosaic text proclaimed the Flood to be a typological "cosmic" reversion back to the time of primeval proto-Earth chaos—which was global.[43] The implication is that the Mosaic author (or, at the very least, the text—whether or not the human author was fully aware of the implications of the text) provides some degree of wider cosmic perspective of reality and is not presenting a narrow regional view of the Noahic Flood. The Flood text would have a weakened theological sense otherwise in the greater historical perspective. This fits the message context of Genesis 1:1, "In the beginning, God created the heavens and the earth" (Hebrew *shamayim eth erets*), which we assert refers to the divine creation of the entire *universe*.[44] In this passage, the Mosaic author connects and sequentially parallels the two words "heavens" (*shamayim*) and "earth" (*erets*) to show a complete and all-encompassing extensiveness in reference to the world (i.e., planetary) with the greater universe.[45] This is a significant postulation when considering the scope of the Flood in light of the inherent connection of the Creation and Flood narratives. It is our conclusion that Hebrew *erets*, as used in Genesis 6–8, should be contextually understood as a global referent, especially in view of its use in Genesis 1:1.

The Hebrew *har*

In consideration of the view that *erets* refers to the planet Earth in the Noahic narrative, it is clearly then a corollary assertion of the text that the Flood waters covered all the Earth's highest elevations (regardless of the height). It

---

of God's creation is followed by God's judgment of cosmic uncreation."; likewise, see Richter, *Epic of Eden*, 144. In concurrence with Davidson and Anderson, Richter calls it a "de-creational event," and adds, "What had been done at creation is undone with the flood. The world is brought back to its pre-creation state—'formless and void.'" Though Richter is a regional Flood advocate, she is implying that the text is presenting a worldwide event image.

43. Note that the Mosaic author would have had no first-hand knowledge of primeval proto-Earth chaos, yet the reversion implication is still inherent to the text. We suggest that this would only be possible if the one who divinely inspired the text (God) was, as a matter of fact, first-hand present during that period of Earth's pre-human natural history.

44. See Stallings, *The Genesis Column*, 56–58.

45. Hasel, "The Biblical View of the Extent of the Flood," 77–95. He states: "The formula 'heaven and earth' which is employed 41 times in the Old Testament and the sequence 'earth and heaven' (6 times) is the standard Hebrew expression for the totality of the world made up of the globe ('earth') and the surrounding atmospheric heavens ('heaven'). It is the Hebrew surrogate for the term 'world' [as in *universe*] (Greek *kosmos*) for which the Hebrew had no single expression" (81).

The Evidence of Scripture

is a common understanding of physical science that water seeks out its own level. Thus, whether a researcher decides to interpret Hebrew *har* as a hill or as a mountain, the basic point is still the same. The globe was completely and at all points covered with water from the Flood.[46] However, providing further supplemental imagery, the addition of the Hebrew *gaboahh* (lit., "high, lofty, tall, elevated," etc.) relating to *har* (the Hebrew text is *kol heharim hugebohim*; lit., "all the high mountains") does seem to lend an emphatic boost to the image of heights a bit more vast than a gentle Mesopotamian hillside.[47] In fact, all things considered, it is quite the textual stretch to interpret otherwise, although a researcher does not have to assume antediluvian mountains to be as high and elevated as the ultra mountains of the present day (e.g., top three prominences: Mt. Everest of China and Nepal—current elev. ^29,000 ft.; Mt. Aconcagua of Argentina—current elev. ^22, 800 ft. ; Mt. McKinley/Denali of Alaska—current elev. ^20,100 ft.; cf. Ps 104:8[48]).[49] Again, the key point is that the text proclaims that the waters of the Noahic Flood covered the highest points across the face of the Earth to a depth of at least fifteen cubits (Gen 7:19–20; fifteen cubits = 22.5 feet). Just how high the mountains at the time of the event may have been is actually an extremely moot point.

THE TEXTUAL PRESENTATION CONCERNING THE UNIQUE DIFFERENCE OF THE NOAHIC FLOOD

Furthermore, there is also great textual significance in the term used for "flood": Hebrew *mabbuwl* (lit., "flood" [in time of Noah][50]). This particular

---

46. See Davidson, "Biblical Evidence," 82–83.

47. Hill, "The Noachian Flood," 173–4. Hill disagrees and presents several reasons why she thinks that Hebrew *har* should not be interpreted as an alpine peak, including: [1] Sumerian ziggurats were sometimes known as a "house of the mountain"; [2] Mesopotamian temple mounds may have been called "mountains" (the Mesopotamian word for "mountain" is derived from "mounds"); and [3] she scoffs at the possibility of Noah trying to measure the depths of the water using a measuring pole if the Flood was "a tempestuous global ocean." The first two thoughts are a mere random grasping at straws; the third is a strawman absurdity (who makes such an assertion?). We conclude that this reasoning is weak and inconclusive and fails to properly interpret the intention of the textual imagery—or recognize its ultimate source.

48. Ps 104:8—"The mountains rose, the valleys sank down to the place which thou didst appoint for them." This verse is part of a *creation* psalm; it thus refers in a very general way to *antediluvian* mountains.

49. We certainly do not believe, however, that the antediluvian mountains were significantly different in elevation than the mountains of today. More on that later.

50. Brown et al., *Hebrew Lexicon*, 550 (H3999).

term is used only thirteen times in the Hebrew Bible. It is found twelve times in Genesis (nine of those directly in the Flood text) and once in the Psalms (Gen 6:17; 7:6, 7, 10, 17; 9:11 [x2], 15, 28; 10:1, 32; 11:10; also, in Ps 29:10). Interestingly, each usage—including that in Psalm 29—arguably refers very specifically to the *Noahic* Flood. The term *mabbuwl*, by its narrow biblical usage, has in effect become a technical term referring to the Noahic Deluge (see Rad, in this note below).[51] The inference is that in the biblical text, the Noahic Flood is supremely differentiated from all other floods that have occurred since the first formation of inhabitable land. As Davidson explains, "This technical term clearly sets the Genesis Deluge apart from all local floods. Psalm 29:10 utilizes it to illustrate Yahweh's universal sovereignty over the world at the time of the Noahic Flood: 'The Lord sat enthroned at the Flood, and the Lord sits as King forever' (NKJV)."[52] Thus, the placement of the Flood in the Lordship context of Psalm 29:10 puts the event in the greater universal perspective and sternly rebukes any local Flood view.[53]

The point is this: No matter how large or devastating that any other floods may have ever been in the many overflows of the Tigris-Euphrates network (as is posited with the typical Mesopotamian Regional Flood model), or any other areas in the whole world, the Noahic Flood was an event that was completely different from any and all other floods—period. Its expansiveness in every way was different and its purpose in every way was different. The Noahic *mabbuwl* was a supreme statement as to divine sovereignty and divine holiness.

Chaffey and Lisle add this summative thought:

51. Esteemed Old Testament scholar, Gerhard von Rad, adds another caveat when he asserts that the Hebrew *mabbuwl* is not actually a regular word for flood. In fact, it does not refer to any sort of normal flood understanding at all, but rather "it is a technical term for a part of the [phenomenological] world structure, namely the heavenly ocean," which carries with it "the same realistic and cosmological ideas as in Gen., ch. 1" (Rad, *Genesis*, 128). This notion is further confirmation of the global Flood image that is inherently built into the biblical text.

52. Davidson, "Biblical Evidence," 83–84.

53. For a slightly dissenting opinion, see Young, *The Biblical Flood*, 3–5. Young comments: "Psalm 29 celebrates the awesome power and control that Yahweh exerts over the created order . . . Although this text may allude to the power of Yahweh displayed in the deluge of Noah, it may perhaps better be understood to refer to the primeval waters of Genesis 1:2. Even if Noah's flood was in view, we learn nothing about the event that we did not already know" (3). We concur with Young's view in the sense that Psalm 29 does indeed allude to the primordial global waters of Genesis 1:2; however, the force of the text is actually in its comparison of the two, and thus the Psalm 29 usage actually serves as an exclamation point to the global Flood concept (i.e., both were global events that demonstrated God's supreme lordship over the universe).

The Evidence of Scripture

> The Old Testament uses a particular word to describe the Flood... . it uses the word *mabbuwl* . . . The Hebrew language has other words, such as *nachal* or *mayim*, to describe the kinds of local floods we see today. It is as if the Hebrew writers were making it very clear that the flood of Noah's day was entirely unique.[54]

This, in fact, is unquestionably the case. The Mosaic author understands the event to be "a catastrophe involving the entire cosmos"[55] from above and from below (i.e., following Rad, this refers to the inundating release of "the heavenly ocean," viz., the cosmic ocean).[56] From a scientific perspective, the prior equilibrium that had been given by God to calm and balance the primordial chaos of the proto-Earth on God Day Three, with the first appearance of stable and permanently inhabitable land,[57] was temporarily disrupted and reversed by the divinely directed release of the surging *mabbuwl*. During this time, all of the land (Hebrew *adamah*) on the face of the planet Earth (Hebrew *erets*), which had been put into place by God for the "very good" ultimate purpose of human inhabitability (humanity is, after all, the Crown of God's creation and is given dominion over that created order), briefly lost all of its previously prepared *inhabitability* via the *mabbuwl* cataclysm.[58] The intended image of the text is that the Earth had been apocalyptically reverted back to a chaotic primeval water world, which to some limited degree was reminiscent of the undeveloped, volatile, and life-incompatible existence of Genesis 1:2.[59] Within the sensibility of the mind of God, this compulsory judgment was potently consistent with the degree of sin present and active within violently evil humanity (see Gen

---

54. Chaffey and Lisle, *Old-Earth Creationism on Trial*, 89.

55. Rad, *Genesis*, 128.

56. Rad elaborates on the imagery: "When the heavenly ocean breaks forth upon the earth below, and the primeval sea beneath the earth, which is restrained by God, now freed from its bonds, gushes up through yawning chasms onto the earth, then there is a destruction of the entire cosmic system according to biblical cosmogony. The two halves of the chaotic primeval sea—the one up, the other below—by God's creative government (ch. 1.7–9), are again united; creation begins to sink again into chaos" (Rad, *Genesis*, 128).

57. See Stallings, *The Genesis Column*, 78–80.

58. Also, do not miss the reality that, during this time, humanity—for cause—had a major portion of its *functional* position of dominion temporarily stripped away by the power of Almighty God.

59. Genesis 1:2 is phenomenologically descriptive of the early proto-Earth—and, therefore, not merely an image of a proto-Mesopotamia. A local or regional event does not square in any way whatsoever with the full textual picture.

6:5–7, 11–13).⁶⁰ This is precisely why the word *mabbuwl* was chosen, rather than ordinary Hebrew flood words such as *mayim*,⁶¹ *sheteph*,⁶² *zerem*,⁶³ or *nachal*,⁶⁴ etc. Thus, the narrow usage of this particular term, along with its contextual reference in Psalm 29:10, provides yet another scriptural sign that the Flood was of global proportions.

THE TEXTUAL PRESENTATION CONCERNING THE UNIVERSAL EMPHASIS OF THE NOAHIC FLOOD

The Usage of Universal Language

In addition to the expansiveness implied by the use of the Hebrew terms *erets* (*Earth*: indicating the wideness of the Flood) and *har* (*mountains*: indicating the depth of the Flood), there is indeed an over-arching universal emphasis implied by the Noahic text as a whole. This is found in multiple key phrases, including the following: [1] Hebrew *al pene kol ha erets*; lit., "upon the face of all the earth" (Gen 7:3 and 8:9); [2] Hebrew *pene ha adamah*; lit., "face of the ground" (Gen 7:4, 22, 23; 8:8, 13); [3] Hebrew *kol basar*; lit., "all flesh" (Gen 6:12, 13, 17, 19; 7:16, 21; 8:17; also found in 9:11, 15, 16, 17); [4] Hebrew *kol*

---

60. Note that the devastation to non-human life is justly based on God's action toward all of that which fallen humankind has dominion. Just as non-human life was consequentially affected by the Adamic Fall, so was non-human life similarly affected by the Noahic Flood. Yet, even in the devastation, divine grace was given in both judgment events enabling humanity, non-human life, and the non-sentient physical order to persist and eventually be renewed.

61. Hebrew *mayim*—"water, waters, flood, pool": Gen 6:17 (used with *mabbuwl*); 7:6 (used with *mabbuhl*), 7:7 (used with *mabbuwl*); 7:10 (used with *mabbuwl*), 7:17 (used with *mabbuwl*); 9:11 (used with *mabbuwl*), 9:15 (used with *mabbuwl*); 2 Sam 5:20; 1 Chr 14:11; Job 22:11; 27:20; 38:34; Pss 69:2, 15; 88:17; 124:4. Note that in those passages where this word is coupled with *mabbuwl*, the construction serves to further intensify the magnitude of the referenced event. See Brown et al., *Hebrew Lexicon*, 555, 565–66 (H4325).

62. Hebrew *sheteph*—"flood, deluge, overflowing of water, [even figuratively for] outrageous": Job 38:25; Ps 32:6; Prov 27:4; Dan 9:26; 11:22; Nah 1:8. See Brown et al., *Hebrew Lexicon*, 1009 (H7858).

63. Hebrew *zerem*—"flood, flood of rain, rainstorm, storm, downpour, tempest, overflow": Job 24:8; Isa 4:6; 25:4[x2]; 28:2[x2]; 30:30; 32:2; Hab 3:10. See Brown et al., *Hebrew Lexicon*, 281 (H2230).

64. Hebrew *nachal*—"torrent": Gen 26:17, 19; 32:23; Lev 11:9, 10; 23:40; Num 13:23, 24; 21:12, 14, 15; 24:6; 32:9; 34:5; Deut 1:24; 2:13[x2], 14, 24; 36[x2], 37; 3:8, 12, 16, etc. Including these listed texts, this word is used a total of 141 times in various forms. See Brown et al., *Hebrew Lexicon*, 636 (H5158).

ha basar; lit., "all the flesh" (Gen 7:15); [5] Hebrew *kol hahay*; lit., "every living thing" (Gen 6:19); [6] Hebrew *kol hayequm*; lit., "all existence" (Gen 7:4, 23); [7] Hebrew *tahat kol hassamayim*; lit., "under the whole heaven" (Gen 7:19; cf. Deut 2:25; 4:19; Job 28:24; 37:3; 41:11; Dan 9:12); and [8] Hebrew *ma yenoth tehom rabbah*; lit., "all the fountains of the great deep" (Gen 7:11; 8:2).[65] The totality of these phrases provides a very strong impetus toward an account referring to a global Flood. Even Hill, who is a regional Flood advocate, sees this as significant. She states: "The best argument, biblically speaking, for a worldwide flood is the 'universal' language used in Gen. 6–8, and this is no doubt the main reason why people in centuries past have believed that Genesis was talking about the planet Earth, and why this traditional interpretation has continued to the day."[66] Hasel concludes:

> The Genesis flood narrative provides ample evidence of being an account which is to be understood as a historical narrative in prose style. It expects to be taken literally. There is a consistent and overwhelming amount of terminology and formulae such as the frequent usages of "earth" and "all the earth," "the face of the ground," "the dry land," "all flesh," "under the whole heaven," which on the basis of context and syntax has uniformly indicated that the flood story wants to be understood in a universal sense: the waters destroyed all human and animal plus bird life on the entire land mass of the globe. To read it otherwise means to force a meaning on the carefully written and specific syntactical constructions of the original language which the text itself rejects.[67]

This means simply that any regional Flood interpretation is a view forced upon the scriptural text against its original intention.

THE NECESSITY OF A GLOBAL FLOOD INTERPRETATION TO THE GREATER THEOLOGICAL CONTEXT

The importance of the Noahic Flood's interpretation goes far beyond itself as a necessary historical event and transcends powerfully into the larger realm of orthodox-evangelical Christian theology. It is actually a pillar by which other significant theological precepts either stand or fall. Therefore, whether

---

65. Davidson, "Biblical Evidence," 81–83. See also Hasel, "The Biblical View of the Extent of the Flood," 3–7.

66. Hill, "The Noachian Flood," 171. Of course, Hill still concludes that this language does "not necessarily have an all-inclusive or universal meaning."

67. Hasel, "The Biblical View of the Extent of the Flood," 7.

the Flood should be understood as regional or global is of utmost importance to grasping the full counsel of God in Christ.

There are several key thoughts that clearly emphasize this point. First, the Flood, when viewed as a global event, fits smoothly into the greater thematic picture of biblical history: viz., the forward flowing themes of creation—re-creation—new creation. Paul F. Taylor concurs:

> Too many Christians today do not understand the central fundamental importance of the Flood to our knowledge of theology.... Creation, Corruption, Catastrophe, Confusion, Christ, Cross, Consummation. Just as the sin of Adam followed creation, and his failure as our first representative, so the catastrophe—the Flood—followed by the judgment of God as a type of the judgment to come at the end of all things.[68]

When the Flood is understood to be a localized event, its place in the greater system of theological understanding becomes critically weakened.

Second, the major themes of Genesis 1–11 (i.e., the creation of the universe, the Fall of humanity, the prophecy of coming redemption, the spread of sin and evil) are all universal in their scope and are all connected to a universal judgment. Consider these several thoughts. [1] The specific terminology used in Genesis 6–8 in reference to the Flood is clearly an allusion to the Genesis 1–2 creation of "the heavens and earth" narrative (which is *very* universal in scope). [2] Likewise, the Adamic Fall issued in the depraved condition of the human race and not merely the local inhabitants of the Mesopotamian region—or, for that matter, any other narrow local or regional territory—at a given point in time. Even to this day, the Adamic Fall is still active and remains universal in scope. [3] Related to the Fall is the divine issuance of the Protoevangelium (Gen 3:15). This speaks of the great moral struggle that would carry on between the "seed" of Satan and the "seed" of humanity, which would ultimately culminate in the representative victory of the Messiah—born through human seed—over the Devil. The redemptive plan of God is universal in scope. [4] Similarly, the ongoing sinful condition of humanity was also not localized to those living in Mesopotamia or any other regional community. The statement of Genesis 6:5 is from the meta-perspective of *God* and not from a local human narrator. The results of his investigative judgment are that the wickedness of humanity (Hebrew *ha dam*) "was great in the earth, and that every imagination of the thoughts of

---

68. Taylor, *The Six Days of Genesis*, 137.

The Evidence of Scripture

his heart was only evil continually." This implies universal human sinfulness requiring universal human judgment.[69]

Third, the divine purpose of the Flood was to bring total judgment upon sinful humanity. In Genesis 6:7, God said, "I will blot out man whom I have created from the face of the ground, man and beast and creeping things and birds of the air, for I am sorry that I have made them." With the exception of Noah and his family (Gen 6:8), the text posits divine judgment aimed at the complete destruction of the human race. According to Davidson, since humanity had minimally existed for over 1,650 years since creation (this is a YEC number), it is highly unlikely that the antediluvian population would have remained only in Mesopotamia.[70] Please note that an OEC timeline of virtually any persuasion would amplify this even more—probably much more.[71] Either way, however, the judgment of Genesis 6:7 would have logically required a global Flood.

Fourth, the genealogical records of Genesis are indicative of the extreme and exclusive ramifications of the Flood. The Flood effectually separated the two patriarchal lineages of humanity (viz., the Adamic lineage of pre-Flood humanity and the Noahic lineage of post-Flood humanity). The text presents a logical universal parallel: Just as from the descendants of Adam came all people on the face of the Earth *before* the Flood (Gen 4:17–26; 5:1–31), from the descendants of Noah came all people on the face of the Earth *after* the Flood (Gen 10:1–32; 11:1–19).[72] This genealogical parallel points to a global distribution of humanity both pre- and post-Flood which thus necessitates a global Flood to accomplish the divine judgment of Genesis 6:7. It is the very pre-Flood population *distribution* that sets the stage for and is mirrored by the post-Flood population *redistribution*.

Fifth, God gave the same expansive command to "be fruitful and multiply" to both Adam (Gen 1:28) and to Noah (Gen 9:1). This provides yet another significant link between the universal creation text and the Noahic Flood text. It shows the very intentional connection between the *beginning* and the *new beginning*. As the original generations of antediluvian humanity began with Adam, the new generations of postdiluvian humanity would

---

69. See Davidson, "Biblical Evidence," 84–85.

70. Davidson, "Biblical Evidence," 86.

71. See Stallings, *The Genesis Column*, 107–30. We hold that humanity has existed since, at least, 1.9 Ma.

72. Davidson, "Biblical Evidence," 86. Please note that Noah is also of Adamic descent.

The Genesis Cataclysm

begin with Noah.[73] Again, this strong parallel points to the necessity of a global Flood.

Sixth, there is a very strong overall parallel between the creation narrative of Genesis 1–2 and the post-Flood "re-creation" narrative of Genesis 8–9. Note the following specific comparatives: [1] there was wind over the waters (Gen 1:2 and Gen 8:1); [2] there was division of the waters (Gen 1:6–8 and Gen 8:1–5); [3] there was the appearance of plants (Gen 1:9–13 and Gen 8:6–12); [4] there was the appearance of light (Gen 1:14–19 and Gen 8:13–14); [5] there was the blessed abundance of animals (Gen 1:20–23 and Gen 8:15–17); [6] there was the connection, yet differentiation, of humanity and animals (Gen 1:24–31 and Gen 8:18–9:7); and [7] there was a divine covenant made with humanity (Gen 2:1–3 and Gen 9:8–17).[74] This is a powerful theological statement linking the *universal* creation text with the Noahic Flood text. The full impact of the linkage can only be logically and emphatically understood if the Flood was a global event.

Seventh, the strategic placement of the Flood in the ordering of the Genesis genealogies must not be missed. As previously mentioned in *The Genesis Column*, there are equally ten generations noted antediluvian and ten generations noted post-diluvian. This clearly marks the Noahic Flood as the *central* feature of pre-Abrahamic human history.[75] This reveals the strong intention of the Mosaic author to give the Flood a universal emphasis.

Eighth, the rainbow covenant that God made with Noah (Gen 9:8–17) after the Flood, which is clearly connected textually to the "whole earth" extent of the Flood,[76] is given to Noah and to all of his descendants (all post-Flood humanity) as well as to all the animals who came off the Ark and to their descendants (Gen 9:9–10): viz., "for all future generations" (Gen 9:12). This emphatically includes its extension to "all flesh" (this phrase is repeated four times; Gen 9:11, 15 [x2], 16) upon the whole Earth. Further, it stands as a sign of "the *everlasting* covenant between God and *every* living creature of *all* flesh that is upon the earth" (Gen 9:16). Fretheim likens the rainbow covenant to that of a "divine oath,"[77] which reinforces the nature of its all-creaturely and all-terrestrial expansiveness and testifies to its unconditional permanence. It is significant that with the Noahic Covenant, God made his divine oath to never again send a worldwide Flood cataclysm, but has

---

73. Davidson, "Biblical Evidence," 86.
74. Doukhan, *The Genesis Creation Story*, 133–34.
75. Stallings, *The Genesis Column*, 107–10.
76. Davidson, "Biblical Evidence," 86.
77. Fretheim, "Genesis," 1:399.

continued to allow for the ongoing occurrence over time of local and regional flood events throughout the world. This means that God has made a clear distinction between the types of events. If the Noahic Flood were anything less than a global event, then the Noahic Covenant—and as such, the *divine oath*—would be abrogated and thus rendered meaningless. However, we need not be concerned over this. God always keeps his oaths and promises. The repetitive usage of universal terminology and the powerful universal emphasis of the covenant itself—definitively linked to the universality of the Flood—is very unmistakable. It should also be added that the divine testimony through the rainbows continues to be proclaimed to this day—by the regular appearance of the rainbows themselves—all over the Earth (globally).[78] Everything about God's oath, God's rainbow, and God's Flood indicates global universality.

Ninth, it is interesting also that the Hebrew *erets* (and not the Hebrew *adamah*; lit., "land" or "ground"), is the term used for "earth" (six times—Gen 9:10, 11, 13, 14, 16, 17) throughout the covenant narrative.[79] This is no accidental or random usage. We contend that this implies the textual intention of a global focus for the Noahic Covenant (which is linked to the global extent of the Noahic Flood). Certainly, the lack of any particular limitation as proclaimed by the Noahic Covenant highlights the lack of any particular limitation as imposed by the Noahic Flood.

Tenth, the Noahic Flood, when understood as a global event, is a *precursory* reversal of original creation followed by an archetypical re-creation culminating in a sort of "new creation."[80] This parallels the *final* eschatological consummation of the Original Relative Creation (viz., the original perfect creation, described as being relative because it was capable of falling) that will be ultimately culminated in the Final Absolute Creation (viz., the final perfect creation, described as being absolute because it will be incapable of falling). Since the Eschaton will be a universal cataclysm, a regional Flood understanding is not a valid theological fit.[81]

---

78. Gen 9:13—[God said] "I set my bow in the cloud, and it shall be a sign of the covenant between me and the earth [Hebrew *erets*]." Also, Gen 9:17—"God said to Noah, 'This is the sign of the covenant which I have established between me and all flesh [Hebrew *kol basar* = "all living things"] that is upon the earth."

79. Hebrew *adamah* is not used at all in the covenant text. This construction is a textual parallel to the creation narrative of Genesis 1:1–2, which is universal and planetary in scope.

80. *Precursory reversal* means a temporary reversal which anticipates the final and permanent reversal yet to come.

81. See Davidson, "The Flood," 262. He states: "The eschatological term *qes* (end)

The Genesis Cataclysm

Davidson provides this closing commentary:

> In conclusion, the question of the extent of the Genesis Flood is not just a matter of idle curiosity with little at stake for the Christian faith.... It is also pivotal in understanding and remaining faithful to the theology of Genesis 1–11 and the rest of Scripture.... [and] serve[s] to theologically connect protology (creation) and eschatology (judgment/salvation) in the opening chapters of Scripture. The Flood is an eschatological step-by-step "uncreation" of the world and humanity followed by a step-by-step "recreation" of the new world.... The theology of the global flood is, therefore, the pivot of a connected but multifaceted universal theme running through Genesis 1–11 and constituting an overarching pattern for the whole rest of Scripture: world-wide creation revealing the character of the Creator and His original purpose for creation; humanity's turning away from the Creator and the universal spread of sin, ending in the universal "uncreation" through universal eschatological judgment; and re-creation, in the eschatological salvation of the faithful covenant remnant and the universal renewal of the earth.[82]

In the spirit of John Warwick Montgomery, the reality of an historical global Flood is absolutely essential to a cogent and systematic understanding of the totality of biblical theology.

THE TEXTUAL PRESENTATION CONCERNING THE NEW TESTAMENT VIEW OF THE NOAHIC FLOOD

How is the Noahic Flood, which is chronicled in the Old Testament, understood within the pages of the New Testament? It is evident that the writers of the New Testament understood a definitive typological connection between the Flood and eschatology. The New Testament message links the Noahic Flood to both the theological concepts of salvation and judgment in the greater schematic of time.

First, the Petrine salvific passage will be examined. 1 Peter 3:18–22 states:

[taken from Genesis 6:13, "end of all flesh"], later became a technical term for the eschaton." This provides substantiation for the textual and theological connection of the two events.

82. Davidson, "Biblical Evidence," 89–90.

The Evidence of Scripture

> For Christ also died for sins once for all, the righteous for the unrighteous, that he might bring us to God, being put to death in the flesh but made alive in the spirit; in which he went and preached to the spirits in prison, who formerly did not obey, when God's patience waited in the days of Noah, during the building of the ark, in which a few, that is, eight persons, were saved through water. Baptism, which corresponds to this, now saves you, not as a removal of dirt from the body but as an appeal to God for a clear conscience, through the resurrection of Jesus Christ, who has gone into heaven and is at the right hand of God, with angels, authorities, and powers subject to him.

In this text, Peter typologically relates the saving of Noah and his family through water (using the Ark) to the New Testament Sacrament of Holy Christian Baptism, which is functionally administered with water (using a font or other reservoir). Please note that Peter is not claiming that the act of Christian Baptism is wholly and finally salvific in and of itself. The point that Peter is making is that the image of water baptism is a means of grace that is associated with salvation by faith in the Risen Christ.[83] With this thought in mind, Peter asserts that salvation through the Flood and salvation through Christ correspond to one another. One is typological of the other. Therefore, since salvation through Christ is a universal offer (2 Pet 3:8–10, esp. v. 9 = "The Lord is . . . not wishing that any should perish, but that all should reach repentance."), then Peter is logically inferring that the Flood (which corresponds to Baptism) was a global phenomenon. Otherwise the analogical typology would critically break down. Note also that Peter places the entire comparative Flood-Baptism typology in the context of Christ's universal Lordship. This further accentuates the global concept of the Flood.

Next, we will examine the passages relating to eschatological judgment. These include the gospel narratives, namely, Matthew 24:37–39, which states:

> As were the days of Noah, so will be the coming of the Son of man. For as in those days before the flood [Greek *kataklysmos*] they were eating and drinking, marrying and giving in marriage,

---

83. Chapman, "The First Epistle of Peter," 2612. Chapman comments: "Technically, of course, it is not true that baptism saves; the merely mechanical performance of the religious rite would only make a sinner into a very wet sinner. . . . What it means is that just as the ark had something to do with the deliverance of those people from the judgment of the Flood, so baptism, assuming that a person has accepted Christ as Savior and desires to obey in this ordinance, has something to do with deliverance from sin. It's only a picture, a type, and the correspondence is very close." (Please note that while Chapman is obviously writing from a non-sacramental perspective, his typological inference is valid from any Christian perspective.)

> until the day when Noah entered the ark, and they did not know until the flood [Greek *kataklysmos*] came and swept them all away, so will be the coming of the Son of man;

and the parallel passage of Luke 17:26–27:

> As it was in the days of Noah, so will it be in the days of the Son of man. They ate, they drank, they married, they were given in marriage, until the day when Noah entered the ark, and the flood [Greek *kataklysmos*] came and destroyed them all.

First of all, in these texts, Jesus—the incarnate Son of God—speaks directly. Please do not miss that he compares the Noahic Flood to the Eschaton within the relative bounds of chronological time (one past, the other future), yet with the certainty of a firsthand witness to *both* events. Second, as mentioned earlier in this chapter, it is deemed to be an ineffective interpretation to see this comparison as merely referring to the suddenness and unexpectedness of the two events. That is only a part of the meaning. We believe that Jesus is also showing a similarity in their expansiveness as well. Note the word for "flood" used in the New Testament text: Greek *kataklysmos*.[84] It is from this word that the English word *cataclysm* is derived. *Cataclysm* is popularly defined as "a great flood; deluge," or "any violent upheaval that causes sudden violent changes, as an earthquake, war, etc."[85] While these definitions in and of themselves do not automatically imply a global event, they do imply a very significant and catastrophic event. However, it is quite striking that the Greek *kataklysmos* is only used four times in the entire New Testament (Matt 24:38, 39; Luke 17:27; 2 Pet 2:5) and each usage is a direct reference to the Noahic Flood. There are other words for "flood" used elsewhere in the New Testament (e.g., Greek *plemmura*[86], Greek *potamos*[87]) that could have been used for the Flood of Noah—but were not. This is a textual scenario similar to the sole Noahic usage of the Hebrew *mabbuwl* in the Old Testament. It is a very emphatic statement by Jesus and by Peter that the Noahic Flood was very different than all other flood events of history. The contextual usage of *kataklysmos* in the New Testament is a clear and supreme proclamation of differentiation.

---

84. Greek *kataklysmos* = "an inundation, deluge" (G2627).
85. See "cataclysm," *Webster's New World Dictionary*, 222.
86. Greek *plemmura* = "a flood, whether of sea or of a river" (G4132). See Luke 6:48.
87. Greek *potamos* = "a stream, a river, a torrent, floods" (G4215). See Luke 6:49 and Rev 12:15, 16.

The Evidence of Scripture

Another important matter is that Jesus would be making an extremely weak Flood/Eschaton comparison if the Noahic Flood were something other than a global event. Since the Eschaton is clearly presented in the Scriptures as a universal event (see, for instance, Rev 1:7—"Behold, he is coming with the clouds, and every eye will see him, every one who pierced him; and all tribes of the earth will wail on account of him.")—both in the magnitude of the event itself and in its wide-ranging chronological awareness—it would behoove all diligent interpreters of Scripture to understand the Flood in a comparable manner. The two events must have a wide cataclysmic commonality in order for the message of Christ in Matthew 24 and Luke 17 to carry maximal typological effectiveness. Otherwise, there would be a degree of absurdity in their comparison. Undoubtedly, the thoughts of Christ as he spoke these words were of a past global Flood catastrophe (involving salvation and judgment) serving as a harbinger of a future universal consummation (involving salvation and judgment).

There are also related eschatological judgment passages from Peter, namely, from 2 Peter 2:5, 9–10, which states,

> [I]f he did not spare the ancient world, but preserved Noah, a herald of righteousness, with seven other persons, when he brought a flood [Greek *kataklysmos*] upon the world of the ungodly . . . then the Lord knows how to rescue the godly from trial, and to keep the unrighteous under punishment until the day of judgment, and especially those who indulge in the lust of defiling passion and despise authority;

and from 2 Peter 3:3–7:

> First of all you must understand this, that scoffers will come in the last days with scoffing, following their own passions and saying, 'Where is the promise of his coming? For ever since the fathers fell asleep, all things have continued as they were from the beginning of creation.' They deliberately ignore this fact, that by the word of God heavens existed long ago, and an earth formed out of water and by means of water, through which the world that then existed was deluged [Greek *kataklyzo*—verb] with water and perished. But by the same word the heavens and earth that now exist have been stored up for fire, being kept until the day of judgment and destruction of ungodly men.

In the 2 Peter 2:5, 9–10 text (above), Peter uses graphic and broadly sweeping language to convey that the judgment of God upon the unrighteous of "the ancient world" (v. 5; Greek *archaios kosmos*: *archaios* = that which has been from the beginning, original, primal, old, ancient[88]; *kosmos* = arrangement or constitution, order, government; adornment, i.e. the arrangement of stars, the heavenly hosts, ornament of the heavens; the world, the universe; the circle of the Earth, the Earth; the inhabitants of the Earth; the whole circle of earthly goods; any aggregate or general collection of particulars of any sort[89]) was complete and total (note also the supplemental use of Greek *kataklysmos* in verse 5). We aver that the contextual connotation of *archaios kosmos* in Peter's usage infers the Earth in its "global" totality, along with all of its antediluvian inhabitants and their corresponding civilization. By using the phrase "ancient world," Peter is speaking in an all-encompassing description. He is asserting that through the Flood judgment, God erased the *entire* antediluvian civilization—people, culture, technology, etc. from the face of the *entire* planet Earth.[90] Ross's incorrect postulation that the entire antediluvian civilization remained in the confines of the Mesopotamian region creates a severe force-fit with the wider intentions of the scriptural message. We believe that Peter would be very shocked and dismayed at the thought of his words being construed and interpreted as referring to a locally regional Noahic Flood.

Moreover, there is clearly both the absolute righteousness and the lavish grace of God evident in the recorded event. In the midst of the total judgment, God saved some (a small faithful remnant) through the Ark. The others (the large unfaithful masses) experienced divine wrath when the Flood inundated the Earth with water and caused them all to perish. From this, Peter subtly alludes to the final eschatological judgment yet to come. God both "knows how to rescue the godly," but also how "to keep the unrighteous under punishment until the day of judgment." The implication

---

88. Mounce, "Ancient," 19–20 (G744).

89. Mounce, "World," 808–809 (G2889).

90. William H. Shea, "The Antediluvians," 10–26. Shea states: "Genesis 3–6 tells of the experiences of some of the earliest members of the human race—those who lived during the interval between creation (as recorded in Genesis 1–2) and the flood (as recorded in Genesis 7–9). From an evolutionary approach to biology, geology, or biblical studies, the "antediluvians" cannot be historical figures. A more direct reading of the biblical text, on the other hand, indicates that the author of these narratives and lists understood them to be historical individuals. The archaeologist cannot assist our search for evidence of their existence, for his spade only works upon the surface of the earth as it was modified by the Noachian flood. Although evidence for antediluvians should lie deeper in the geologic strata, geologists have not yet produced such evidence" (10). Shea is correct in his overall point. The antediluvians find their greatest witness in the Holy Scriptures. However, it must be reiterated that there are strong trace evidences (i.e., OOPARTS, etc.) that seem to substantiate not only the existence of an antediluvian society, but an advanced antediluvian civilization. For further, see *The Genesis Column*, 118–30.

is that the Flood judgment, though complete and total, was not the ultimate Day of Judgment (see Rev 20:11–15). *That day* (Matt 24:36–37[91]) is still chronologically yet to come. Those who perished in the Deluge have not completed their adjudication; they will yet stand before God at the Eschaton.[92] Like Jesus, Peter places the precursory Noahic Flood judgment of the past as a type of the final universal judgment event (Eschaton) that is still set to occur in the future. The full intended comparative (Flood-Eschaton / global-universal) is significant and should not be missed.

In the 2 Peter 3:3–7 text (above), Peter continues the image of the Flood-Eschaton typology by making the unmistakable comparison between those in his day who were scoffing at the thought of Christ's return (vv. 3–4) and those in Noah's day who scoffed at the thought of a great Flood (v. 6). He reminds the Christian believers that just as God created the heavens and the Earth (a prior universal event) and just as God inundated that same Earth with the Flood (a prior global event), God will also conclude the same existing universe with fire (a future universal event). Since God created this universe by his Word (John 1:1–3 = Greek *logos*) and caused the Flood by his Word (2 Pet 3:5–6 = Greek *logos*), he will likewise conclude the universe by his Word (2 Pet 3:7 = Greek *logos*; Rev 19:11–16 = Greek *logos*). As Chapman asserts:

> Creation was by the Word of God; the sky, the dry land, and the water were distinguished by the Word of God (Gen. 1:6–7, 9), and the world continues to exist by the Word of God (cf. Col. 1:17 where the same word is used for Jesus Christ as the Living Word of God in exactly the same sense of sustaining the world). . . . According to Peter's analogy here, water and the Word were involved in the destruction of the world by the Flood according to verse 6. With pungent success comes the reply to those satirists who dared to suggest that God would not keep His promise of the Second

---

91. Matt 24:36–37—Jesus said, "But of *that day* and hour no one knows, not even the angels of heaven, nor the Son, but the Father only. As were the days of Noah, so will be the coming of the Son of man" (italics mine).

92. It is very interesting to note that John, in describing his vision of the dead lining up at the Great White Throne judgment, very specifically states in Revelation 20:13: "And *the sea gave up the dead in it*, Death and Hades gave up the dead in them, and all were judged by what they had done" (italics mine). One can wonder if this seemingly very specific and unique rendering about certain unrecovered nautical dead might actually be a veiled reference to those who died in the Noahic Flood, especially in light of the all-encompassing statement about "Death and Hades" included in the same passage (which, of course, in and of itself, already includes *all* dead of *all* time). This could be yet another Flood/Eschaton parallel.

Coming: by the same Word of God, this word is kept in store. . . . It is as clear as Peter can make it that God's Word will certainly be fulfilled in this matter as it has been in others, the second coming and the day of judgment will transpire exactly as promised, and these ungodly men [those who scoff at God's truth] will be destroyed![93]

In this narrative, Peter accentuates both the surety of God's claims and the extensiveness of his work amidst the universal Lordship of Christ. In so doing, Peter textually sandwiches the Flood in between the two universal events of creation and consummation. This sends an extremely strong message concerning the nature of the Flood as presented by the biblical record. (Note also these expansive usages throughout the text: "all things," "creation," "heavens," "and an earth," "the world," "the heavens and earth," and the Greek verb *katakluzo*, "deluged.") When viewed in context, it is not a sensible conclusion to extrapolate that the Noahic Flood was merely regional, and not completely global. If that were the case, the Petrine analogy and language would be very weak, out of place, and woefully inconsistent.

---

93. Chapman, "First Epistle of Peter," 2625–26.

3

The Evidence of Nature

> For the creation waits with eager longing for the revealing of the sons of God; for the creation was subjected to futility, not of its own will but by the will of him who subjected it in hope; because the creation itself will be set free from its bondage to decay and obtain the glorious liberty of the children of God. We know that the whole creation has been groaning in travail together until now; and not only the creation, but we ourselves.[1]

It is important to now look at the fallen natural order to discern what evidence, if any, can be found to substantiate anything concerning the Noahic Flood event. Despite the murkiness and the blur of the decayed and decaying natural order, we will search for some sort of blemished empirical footprint, regardless of just how distinct or faint it may be, in the earthen record. Even with the preeminence of the evidence of Scripture, we believe that this is still a necessary task in order to complete a whole and unabridged investigation. According to Young:

> No study of the relationship between Scripture and earth history would be complete without a consideration of the role of Noah's flood in geological history.... The story is not only very impressive as an account of God's judgment upon the sin of a wicked world but also as a description of an apparently significant geological phenomenon.... The report of Noah's flood has, perhaps more than any other story in the Bible, exercised men's imaginations.

---

1. Rom 8:19–23a.

> The flood story has, of course, been regarded as pure myth but generally is seen as having roots in some historical event. In the Bible-believing world the flood story has always been accepted as a true account of a real, historical phenomenon.[2]

The search for the evidence of nature will be attempted both from a broad and from a narrow perspective.

A word of caution. As we begin to examine the natural order, may we do so, not with arrogance or haste, but with great humility, deep patience, and earnest truth seeking. We would all be quite wise to tread lightly as we explore. For in our striving to see and to understand just what God's creation still has to tell us about something so seemingly impenetrable and (even) cryptic as the Noahic Flood, we must realize at the onset that there are many things in the evidence of nature concerning this occurrence that do not now remain patently clear, overtly neat, and easily discernable. In reality, only the ardent and intensely focused student of the event—and one truly following Christ, who is the Lord of truth himself, as well as one truly seeking first the Kingdom of God and his righteousness—will likely see more than some sort of an indiscriminate mixture in the natural order. Like us, the mixture itself is fallen and marred (see Rom 8:19–23a; described here variously by Paul as being "subjected to futility," as being in "bondage to decay," and "groaning in travail") and requires the clarifying lens of heaven. Thus, parsing out the variant elements of this mixture as tarnished nature presents it will demand much effort and divine leadership. It is one investigative task that requires its sleuths to have the eyes of an eagle (to see), the heart of a lion (to persevere), the light of the Scriptures (to stay veridical), and most importantly of all, the guiding wisdom of the Holy Spirit (to illumine and confirm seemingly disparate connections). Yet, as it always is concerning the mysterious things of God, the treasure trove of truth can be great for those who are willing to carry on humbly, but steadily, in the seeking and in the finding. We encourage all such researchers to stay the course.

Moving forward, it is important to note that our primary intention is not to devise a new theory of Flood mechanics or to justify any particular existing Flood theory. Our purpose is to search for and to study extant evidence of a potential diluvial nature in order to determine whether or not a global Flood can be empirically justified within a particular Old-Earth scriptural paradigm. Certainly, the Noahic Flood, as presented in Genesis, is fraught with elements of both supernatural primary causation (the initiating

---

2. Young, *Creation and the Flood*, 171. Note that Young was once a global Flood advocate, but no longer holds that view.

proclamation of God: "I will bring a flood of waters upon the earth"—Gen 6:17) and natural secondary causation (the responsive action within the created order: "all the fountains of the great deep burst forth, and the windows of the heavens were opened"—Gen 7:11). However, it is our contention that the most important thing for a Christian apologist is to be able to show the reasonable plausibility of its historical occurrence (not to devise or speculate on a mechanistic explanation of secondary causation). We say this with the strong scriptural understanding that God is indeed the direct primary causation (see Gen 6:6–7, 17; 7:16; 8:1–3), regardless of the natural secondary mechanism used. With the Flood being an act of God, it is even possible—we believe probable—that the natural inducing mechanism itself may no longer be extant or identifiable. We will, however, briefly survey the major mechanistic models to show the direction of scholarly thought in this area.

THE OVERVIEW OF PROMINENT GLOBAL FLOOD MODELS

There are many Christian scholars who seek detailed explanations for the mechanism that was the secondary causation of the Flood. The theorists typically come to the matter from the differing perspectives of meteorology, hydrology, geology, astronomy, tectonics, or some combination. Over the years, many theories have been posited,[3] including the following four basic global Flood models[4] that are probably the most currently prominent (each of which has multiple sub-variations, inclusive of the frequent overlap and blending of concepts): [1] the Water/Vapor Canopy Model (e.g., Isaac Newton Vail[5], Robert W. Woods[6], Joseph C. Dillow[7], Larry Vardiman[8]); [2] the

---

3. For a good historical run-down of this, see various sections in Young, *The Biblical Flood*.

4. We have synthesized the many theories into four basic groupings (models). The advocates presented with each model are a representative sampling and are not exhaustive.

5. Vail, *The Earth Annular System*, vi-viii. Vail also makes this astounding comment concerning his confident advocacy of the canopy model: "To endeavor to prove the truth of the theory that supposes this earth to have been, from the close of the igneous era till the close of the antediluvian period, surrounded by an annular system, seems to me, since I have been so long gathering in the fund of evidence, like trying to establish a self-evident truth" (13).

6. Woods, "How Old is the Earth?," 8–9, 15. Here Woods equates the biblical notion of "the waters above the firmament" as a water canopy surrounding the Earth.

7. Dillow, *The Waters Above*.

8. Vardiman, "Temperature Profiles for an Optimized Water Vapor Canopy," 1–11.

Flood Geology Model (e.g., Whitcomb & Morris[9], Andrew A. Snelling[10], Bernard E. Northrup[11], Paul Taylor[12], Paul Garner[13], Gerhard F. Hasel[14], John Woodmorappe,[15] etc.); [3] the Astral Catastrophism Model (e.g., Immanuel Velikovsky[16], Donald Wesley Patten[17]); and [4] the Catastrophic Plate Tectonics Model (e.g., Steven A. Austin, John R. Baumgardner, D. Russell Humphreys, Andrew A. Snelling, Larry Vardiman, Kurt P. Wise[18]).

Note that many mainstream scientists have little or no regard for Noahic Flood models (sometimes even referring to such thinking as "crackpot science"), or often even less regard for the possibility that a global Flood (or, for some, any form of the Flood at all) actually occurred at some point in the distant past. However, as previously asserted in the last chapter, we assume the historicity of the Noahic Flood on biblical grounds; therefore, for the purposes of this project, that case is closed. And furthermore, for the purposes of this project, each of these theoretical models—regardless of any agreement or disagreement with their postulations—are understood to represent a very honorable endeavor in the quest for truth and are considered to be an exercise of the divine dominion mandate. Each theoretical Flood model will be presented as fairly and concisely as possible. For those of us who are Christians, we should remember to always apply both honesty and humility, as we ourselves seek truth and observe others around us doing the same; for at the final consummation of the New Kingdom and the revelation of a greater fullness of reality, we may all find ourselves quite surprised by a lot of things (1 Cor 13:12).[19]

With that in mind, though it is not our primary intention to speculate on a particular Flood theory, it would be a severe act of omission not to briefly describe the basic gist of these four general models. This will be done so that a richer understanding of Flood dynamics can be clearly presented.

9. Whitcomb and Morris, *The Genesis Flood*.
10. Snelling, *Earth's Catastrophic Past* (2 vols.).
11. Northrup, "The Geological Foundation Below the Noahic Flood Deposits."
12. Taylor, *Six Days of Genesis*, 158.
13. Garner, "Geology and the Flood," 1–15.
14. Hasel, "The Fountains of the Great Deep," 67–72.
15. Woodmorappe, *Studies in Flood Geology*.
16. Velikovsky, *Earth in Upheaval*.
17. Patten, *The Biblical Flood and the Ice Epoch*.
18. Austin et al., "Catastrophic Plate Tectonics," 1–12.
19. 1 Cor 13:12—"For now we see in a mirror dimly, but then face to face. Now I know in part; then I shall understand fully, even as I have been fully understood."

For our purposes, such an understanding of proposed mechanisms is helpful in order to be able to more effectively identify possible extant evidence.

The Water/Vapor Canopy Model

The Water/Vapor Canopy Model is the postulation that the early Earth was surrounded by a thick cover ("canopy") of atmospheric water (liquid, vapor, or ice). Advocates often equate the canopy with the waters above the "firmament" or "expanse" mentioned in Genesis 1:6–7 (contrasted with the waters below the firmament or expanse on the Earth's surface). While there are many variations of this theory, the basic idea for them all is that the water came down from the canopy at the onset of the Noahic Flood and contributed to the fluidic covering of the planet. Perhaps the most interesting variation comes from Isaac Newton Vail. Rather than being one large contiguous mass, Vail advocated that the canopy, similar to the conditions of Saturn, consisted of annular rings of water. It was his view that the rings broke one-by-one over vast periods of time with the breaking of the final ring corresponding with the time of the Noahic Deluge.[20]

The Flood Geology Model

The Flood Geology Model is the view that became very prominent among evangelical Christians with the publication of *The Genesis Flood* by Whitcomb and Morris in 1961.[21] The primary emphasis of this model is that the two-fold mechanism of the Noahic Flood mentioned in Genesis 7:11, that is, the bursting forth of *the fountains of the great deep* along with the opening of *the windows of heaven*, is understood to have caused the majority of the current crustal conditions of the Earth.[22] Taylor provides this somewhat typical Flood Geology commentary:

> 20. Vail, *The Earth Annular System*, vi.
> 21. Tyler, "Flood Models and Trends in Creationist Thinking," 1. Tyler comments: "The revival of Flood Geology in the 20th Century owes much to the publication of *The Genesis Flood* in 1961, by John Whitcomb and Henry Morris. Since then, numerous creationist writers and speakers have acknowledged their debt to this book, and most have developed their own thinking to harmonize with that presented by Whitcomb and Morris. This Flood model, in turn, drew in part on the writings of George McCready Price earlier this century [20th century]" (1).
> 22. Tyler, "Flood Models and Trends in Creationist Thinking," 1–5. Tyler presents three different points in the geologic record that various advocates of the Flood Geology Model claim that the Flood may have occurred. They include: [1] the "End-Pliocene

45

> There is no doubt that there was much rain in the Flood. However, the bulk of the Flood waters must have come from another source. . . . the idea of vast underground flows of water—the fountains of the deep. If these fountains existed, then they must have been completely destroyed. Genesis 7:11 suggests that these fountains were indeed a major source of Flood water. In order to break this immense pre-diluvian hydrology, there must have been substantial seismic and volcanic events for the first time in earth's history. These would have broken open these fountains, and produced the dust required for raindrops to form. This rain would be substantial. Genesis describes it as "the windows of heaven" being opened. . . . It is worth emphasizing that the Flood was a worldwide event. Such a major catastrophe would have completely reshaped the earth's crust.[23]

According to this general theory, the bursting of the fountains involved massive subterranean hydrological force, seismic action, and worldwide volcanism; the opening of the windows of heaven involved torrential rainfall—possibly tied to the downward return of water from the exploding fountains and/or the fall of water from the breaking open of the atmospheric canopy—and tremendous erosion.[24] Hasel adds further that the phrase "fountains of the great deep" (Hebrew *tehom* = "deep" can refer to oceans) may hint at the strong role of the pre-Flood oceans and sub-oceanic aquifers in the incredible force of the Deluge.[25] The Flood Geology Model essentially posits that the existing geologic column with its corresponding faunal successions (often interpreted in this model as ecological zonations[26]), modern orogeny

---

Flood model" (1–4), [2] the "End-Cretaceous Flood model" (4–5), and [3] the "End-Carboniferous Flood model" (5). Of course, though he uses standard geological terms to identify the points, each of these postulations disregards the standard deep time interpretation of the geologic column.

23. Taylor, *Six Days of Genesis*, 158.

24. Whitcomb and Morris, *The Genesis Flood*, 7–9, 120–23. For an interesting variation of Flood Geology, see Brown, *In the Beginning*, 105–42. Brown proposes the Hydroplate Theory, which essentially holds that massive amounts of pressurized water trapped below the antediluvian Earth's crust burst forth when the crust weakened due to many centuries of "tidal pumping."

25. Hasel, "The Fountains of the Great Deep," 2–3. Patten concurs with this conclusion (although from a different model perspective); see *The Biblical Flood and the Ice Epoch*, 62–63.

26. See Clark, *Fossils, Flood, and Fire*, 51–60. He explains: "This order of [faunal] succession we might designate as ecological zonation, meaning a series of zones indicating the original ecological, or habitat relationships. This interpretation, then, is suggested as a substitute for the commonly accepted theory of geological ages. In other words, an

(mountain building), and continental movement were the result of massive lithospheric upheaval and cataclysmic flood sedimentation.[27] In other words, the conditions of the terrestrial planet as they appear today were largely caused by the Noahic Flood (and today's version of Earth—including its natural processes—are vastly different from the antediluvian version).

The Astral Catastrophism Model

The Astral Catastrophism Model proposes an astronomical mechanism. This model asserts that interstellar space is replete with many astral bodies in motion on various orbital patterns (some regular, some irregular). Many of these bodies (e.g., asteroids, comets, etc.) are substantial in size and make periodic visitations near the Earth. According to Patten, there are extant evidences of past astral catastrophism in our Solar System. These include the following: [1] cometary origination in the Solar System; [2] the disarrangement or perturbation of moons (e.g., Neptune's moons: Nereid and Triton); [3] the planetary opposition of Neptune and Pluto; [4] the fragmentation of moons (e.g., the many fragments caught in the rings of Saturn); [5] the fragmentation of planets (e.g., the asteroids of Ceres, Juno, Pallas, etc.); and [6] the presence of craters and an arcuate mountain alignment on the Moon.[28] The theory of Astral Catastrophism posits that an astral body "visiting" very

---

"age" of time would be replaced by a "stage" of Flood action" (58).

27. See Northrup, "The Geological Foundation Below the Noahic Flood Deposits," 1. He asserts that there were *three* great catastrophes in the history of the Earth—the covering of the planet with the "original universal flood" after its creation, the raising of "the great single continent in the third solar day of creation," and then only later, the Noahic Flood. According to Northrup: "It is concluded that both the Biblical record and the geological record point specifically to two largely forgotten geological catastrophes in the earth's early events. It is proposed that the entirely non-fossiliferous metamorphosed Archaeozoic deposits record the original universal flood which covered the earth after its creation as the Lord prepared earth's surface for man's habitation. The fierce contortion of its largely sedimentary deposits into the contorted folds is attributed to the abrupt violence of the uplift of the great single continent in the third solar day of creation. This abrupt uplift is identified as the second major catastrophic, geological event which is found in biblical history. It is proposed that this very brief Biblical event and the long-quieting disturbance of the crust of the earth and its shallow sea left the vast section of the Precambrian geological record which is given the name "Proterozoic" by many geologists" (1). In this understanding, all stratification found above the Precambrian/Cambrian boundary was caused by the Noahic Flood and everything below the boundary are the extant remains of what was formed by God during the six solar day (144-hour) Creation Week.

28. Patten, *The Biblical Flood and the Ice Epoch*, 35–36.

close to the Earth became the mechanism of Noahic Flood causation. Patten's very detailed model will be used as an example.

According to Patten's postulation, Mars (whose normal orbital pattern had been elongated and narrowed by the influence of Jupiter) once passed by the Earth rather closely (probably between 15,000–30,000 miles from the Earth's core[29]). Rather than a very short temporary grazing of the Earth's gravitational field, Mars—with an ice-ball satellite (Glacis) in tow—became involved with the Earth-Moon system for a period of several months. As Mars remained nearby, the constitution of the Earth agitated, writhed, and convulsed in geophysical agony. The Martian visit caused massive tidal upheavals (involving both surficial water and internal magma),[30] horizontal and vertical mountain uplifts across the crust,[31] and simultaneous glaciogenesis at the magnetic poles (leading to the Ice Age).[32] Patten explains the two key features of this particular Martian flyby encounter (there were allegedly many over the course of millennia): the tidal effects and the glacial effects. First, the tidal (and corresponding orogenic) effects:

> The extremely close flyby of Mars caused a variety of gigantic changes on the Earth. Mars, one tenth the mass of the Earth, passed over only 15,000 miles distant from the Earth's core and perhaps even less. At that close distance, subcrustal tides would be over 10,000 feet high. The last great cycle of mountain-building does exhibit a swath-like, or a flyby-like pattern. It is the great Alpine-Himalayan cycle, some 12,500 miles long. It spans New Guinea, Indonesia, Southern Asia, Southern Europe, and North Africa. The force uplifting this mountain cycle was vertical (Mars

---

29. Patten, *The Biblical Flood and the Ice Epoch*, 148; also, *Catastrophism and The Old Testament*, 32. He seems to favor a proximity of less than 15,000 miles.

30. Patten, *The Biblical Flood and the Ice Epoch*, 51–64. Patten says, "[T]he Flood was tidal in perspective, the reaction to a gravitational conflict, an astral intruder being the mechanical cause. Oceans would begin to heave and surge in tidal movement; so also would the fluid magma (lava) within the crust of the Earth begin to surge, for all fluids would respond to the gravitational conflict" (64).

31. Patten, *The Biblical Flood and the Ice Epoch*, 65–100. He states: "As Job suggested, the 'pillars of the Earth trembled.' With each approach, a new zone of horizontal uplift occurred (the Circum-Pacific first; the Alpine-Himalayan second). And with each rotation during crisis, there occurred a new range of horizontal uplift, or a further movement of a prior uplift [vertical]. Series after series of sediment was simultaneously deposited and/or compressed (93). He also notes that the lunar mountains have similar patterns with Earth and thus suggest simultaneous orogenesis (90–91). This would be expected if Patten's astral model is correct.

32. Patten, *The Biblical Flood and the Ice Epoch*, 101–136. See also *Catastrophism and the Old Testament*, 34–35.

overhead).... Similar tides from the oceans swept Eurasia, from the Arctic Ocean, from the Pacific Ocean and especially from the Indian Ocean, an ocean containing 75 million cubic miles of water. A significant percent of these waters, around 5%, were pulled up and northward, across India, Iran and the region of Ararat.[33]

Second, the glacial effects:

A second feature of this flyby scene was the fragmentation of an ancient satellite of Mars, an ice ball. At some time in the past, an ice ball had come too close to Saturn and fragmented. So it was on this particular flyby, the closest of them all. Mars must have had an icy satellite (Glacis) which pierced the Earth's Roche Limit, at 11,000 miles, and fragmented. The composition of the ice ball seems to have included traces of the rare element, iridium. This ice ball fragmented, spraying both planets [Earth and Mars].... ice particles and fragments were trapped by the Earth's gravitational field, something like Saturn's rings. The icy fragments gradually turned to icy powder due to the effect of the solar radiation and began to flow in space along field force lines of the geomagnetic field. As extremely cold icy powder, they began to sift down over the two magnetic polar regions, at temperatures around -300° F. Their volume was 12 to 14 million cubic miles of ice.[34]

In this model, the Noahic Flood event was the biblically-reported symptom of the massive tidal effects and correspondent orogenesis occurring across the planet Earth (mechanistically brought about by the Mars encounter). Additionally, Patten asserts that the Ice Age, though not mentioned in Scripture, also was initiated by the Mars encounter at the same time as the Flood. Furthermore, according to Patten's model, Mars remained in a catastrophic orbit and regularly conflicted with Earth every fifty-four years from about 9900 B.C. until 701 B.C.[35] At that point, Mars changed to its current orbital pattern and ceased to interact with Earth. Interestingly, Patten theorizes that these Earth-Mars conflicts of the past were the causal mechanism for numerous biblical phenomena, including "The Long Day of Joshua" (Josh 10:13; cf. Hab 3:11) in 1404 B.C.[36] and the devastating defeat of Sennacherib by "the Angel of the Lord" (2 Kgs 18:1–19; cf. Isa 36–39) in 701

---

33. Patten, *Catastrophism and the Old Testament*, 32–34.
34. Patten, *Catastrophism and the Old Testament*, 34–35.
35. Patten, *Catastrophism and the Old Testament*, 111.
36. Patten, *Catastrophism and the Old Testament*, 132–49.

B.C.[37] The Noahic Flood, which Patten places at the Mars-Earth interaction of 2484 B.C., coincided with the time that Mars came the closest to Earth (due to the influence of Saturn on the Martian orbital pattern) and was thus the most cataclysmic of all the encounters.[38] If nothing else, the Astral Catastrophism Model is fascinating.

The Catastrophic Plate Tectonics Model

The Catastrophic Plate Tectonics Model proposes a tectonic mechanism based on rapid sea-floor subduction.[39] This model was first presented by John R. Baumgardner in 1986 at the First International Conference on Creationism.[40] Austin et al. (Baumgardner included) presents the basic idea:

> The Flood was initiated as slabs of oceanic floor broke loose and subducted along thousands of kilometers of pre-Flood continental margins. Deformation of the mantle by these slabs raised the temperature and lowered the viscosity of the mantle in the vicinity of the slabs. A resulting thermal runaway of the slabs through the mantle led to meters-per-second mantle convection. Cool oceanic crust which descended to the core/mantle boundary induced rapid reversals of the earth's magnetic field. Large plumes originating near the core/mantle boundary expressed themselves at the surface as fissure eruptions and flood basalts. Flow induced in the mantle also produced rapid extension along linear belts throughout the sea floor and rapid horizontal displacement of continents. Upwelling magma jettisoned steam into the atmosphere causing intense global rain. Rapid emplacement of isostatically lighter mantle material raised the level of the ocean floor, displacing ocean water onto the continents.[41]

As to the conclusion of the cataclysm, they add: "When virtually all of the pre-Flood oceanic floor had been replaced with new, less-dense, less-subductable, oceanic crust, catastrophic plate motion stopped. Subsequent

---

37. Patten, *Catastrophism and the Old Testament*, 219–52.
38. Patten, *Catastrophism and the Old Testament*, 112.
39. *Subduction* is a process by which one edge of a crustal plate is forced downward under the edge of another. As this occurs, the subducted crust (lithosphere) can break into large slabs that descend into the Earth's mantle.
40. See Baumgardner, "Numerical Simulation," 1–10.
41. Austin et al., "Catastrophic Plate Tectonics," 1.

cooling increased the density of the new ocean floor, producing deeper ocean basins and a reservoir for post-Flood oceans."[42]

In essence, the idea is that large slabs of sea-floor in the pre-Flood ocean began to rapidly sink (through subduction) into the Earth's mantle at the continental margins. These lithospheric slabs were cold and hard and were probably as much as 100 kilometers thick.[43] As the sea-floor subducted into the hot mantle (which is made up of silicate rock in the form of viscous fluid), the slabs caused a great thermal increase and a lowered viscosity of the mantle silicates. This rapid lithospheric subduction would then have caused great upheaval in the deep recesses of the planet that translated into cataclysmic effects on the Earth's crust.

With this model, there are several possible consequences to runaway subduction that would be contributory to the Flood catastrophe. First, there would have been a great rise in the global sea level relative to the continental lithosphere. The ocean bottom would have thermally expanded upward as hot mantle rock displaced the old sub-oceanic lithosphere that had dropped down to the mantle/core boundary. Second, there would have been incredibly violent tidal waves raging across the Earth. These would have been caused by the intensification of seismic activity affiliated with lithospheric disruption and subduction. Third, there would have been massive volcanic activity, particularly of a sub-aqueous nature, since that is where the lithospheric slabs were coming apart and being filled with magma from the mantle. Fourth, there would have been vertical upheaval of the continental regions as well. As the lithospheric slabs subducted at the continental margins, the viscous drag of the slabs would depress the surface height of the continental seams resulting in massive back-arc spreading (and even supercontinent tearing).[44]

Concerning the "trigger" that would have caused the rapid, subduction process to begin in the first place, Baumgardner makes this suggestion:

> [I]t seems evident that the Flood catastrophe cannot be understood or modeled in terms of time-invariant laws of nature. Intervention by God in the natural order during and after the catastrophe appears to be a logical necessity.... Although many scientists do not readily entertain such possibility, Scripture indicates that God has indeed on rare occasions intervened in the laws of nature on a grand scale. 2 Peter 3:3–6 states that one of these occasions was during the Flood.[45]

---

42. Austin et al., "Catastrophic Plate Tectonics," 1.
43. Baumgardner, "Numerical Simulation," 3.
44. Baumgardner, "Numerical Simulation," 4.
45. Baumgardner, "Numerical Simulation," 9.

These Models as Viewed from the Old-Earth Perspective

From an OEC perspective, the immediate major difficulty with each of these global Flood models is that they are all predicated upon a Young-Earth scenario. All of them present views, particularly those of a geological nature, that go directly against the majority view of modern science in many ways.[46]

The Flood Geology Model claims that the Earth has only an appearance of age and maturity, but is really very young. It also claims that virtually all of the Earth's crustal conditions, including its strata and faunal successions, were caused by the Flood and thus no valid projections can be made about the pre-Flood geological past from current natural processes.[47] We find that this clean wipe of modern geology is a problematic and unrealistic approach to the empirical record.

Meanwhile, the Water/Vapor Canopy Model is pure speculation. Advocates of this idea seem to automatically equate the firmament of Genesis with some form of massive atmospheric or interstellar water containment that was suddenly released on the Earth with the opening of the windows of heaven. The problem with this is that there is no evidence whatsoever that a canopy as such ever existed around the Earth, or that it would have had significant Flood impact. Furthermore, it has been suggested that the antediluvians could not have survived the surface temperatures under such a canopy.[48] Objectively, there is no way to either confirm nor deny.

The Astral Catastrophism Model, while quite colorful and intriguing and perhaps incorporating some valid astrophysics, seems to be more akin to a Gene Roddenberry saga than a plausible possibility. On the other hand, Roddenberry's imagination has been attributed to inspiring a number of scientific breakthroughs. So, perhaps there are nuggets of truth present in this subject area of which further scientific research can ultimately develop. For the time being though—besides God and the holy angels, who else really knows?

---

46. While this, in itself, is not automatically a death knell (after all, theoretically, mainstream science could be incorrect), it does show an almost blanket disregard for a whole body of work from multiple generations of scientific practitioners, many of whom were and are followers of Christ and adherents to the Holy Scriptures. Our point is this: Just as scientific orthodoxy is wrong to give a blanket ejection of Christian and creationist perspectives from due consideration, so too is Christian and creationist orthodoxy wrong in doing the same with the advocations of mainstream science. Both extremes are obstacles to finding truth wherever it can be found.

47. Whitcomb and Morris, *The Genesis Flood*, 228.

48. See Morton, "The Demise and Fall of the Water Vapor Canopy."

The Evidence of Nature

The Catastrophic Plate Tectonics Model does, in certain places, have some good scientific logic attached, but seems to have as its first order of business the automatic justification of a YEC paradigm instead of the straightforward interpretation of the extant *as is* geological record. Since, according to the majority-position of modern science, the visible rock record most plausibly shows the result of geologic processes occurring over great periods of deep time interspersed with some signs of catastrophism, this model seems to have been created as a way to show that an apparent lack of visible and permanent worldwide diluvial stratigraphic evidence is actually *the* evidence of a worldwide Deluge. This it shares somewhat in common with the Flood Geology Model. However, one of the most important features of this concept involves subducted lithospheric slabs. This phenomenon will indeed later come back into the discussion, but in another manner.

For the most part, each of the models concludes with a world that has been completely changed from (at least) the upper mantle boundary to the crust[49] and is thus drastically different in virtually every way from its antediluvian "predecessor." While the Noahic Flood was an act of divine judgment primarily on fallen, evil humanity, and secondarily upon the fallen world in which evil humanity existed and had dominion, this enormous degree of proposed *terrestrial* change seems to be a bit more than what the Holy Scriptures present as actually being the case. For instance, both the Tigris and the Euphrates rivers exist both pre- (see Gen 2:10-14) and post-Flood (see Gen 15:18; Dan 10:4).[50] In fact, both rivers still exist today—and, at least, the Euphrates[51] will continue to exist until the time of God's final judgment (Rev 16:12), if not beyond. If the crustal formation

---

49. Note that it is possible for a variation of the Canopy Model to advocate for a somewhat tranquil Flood, although most modern proponents of a canopy connect it to a variation of the Flood Geology Model—which is typically understood to be geologically catastrophic and Earth-changing in the most extreme possible manner.

50. As an additional caveat, we know that another of the four great Edenic rivers of Genesis 2, the Gihon River (first mentioned at Gen 2:13 in the creation narrative), also existed during the time of David and Solomon (see 1 Kgs 1:33, 38, 45), who ruled Israel from approximately 970–931 B.C., as well as during the time of Hezekiah (see 2 Chr 32:30; 33:14), who ruled Judah from approximately 715–686 B.C. This, of course, means that some form of the Gihon existed both pre-Flood and significantly post-Flood—although we are not *absolutely* certain as to whether or not it still exists to this day under, perhaps, a different designation and form. This matter will be briefly discussed in a later footnote.

51. Note that the Euphrates River is mentioned five times in the Bible (Gen 2:14, 15:18; Josh 1:4; Rev 9:14, 16:12) ranging from Genesis through Revelation. On the other hand, the Tigris River is only mentioned in the Bible twice—in Genesis 2:14 (the only text where the Tigris and Euphrates are mentioned together) and in Daniel 10:4.

of the Earth were so completely, deeply, and drastically changed by the Noahic Flood, then it seems strange that those rivers—or any such pre-existing landmarks at all—would still be around after the event. Of course, this should serve as an alert to us; instead of dealing with the plainly visible empirical conditions and processes available at the current time (which, though fallen, is what we have to work with; and which is also, by the way, a direct snub of the standard uniformitarian mantra, "the present is the key to the past") and then developing logical and plausible scripturally-framed conclusions from there, these Flood models seem to be presenting a sort of arbitrary argument from "silence" that probably cannot be tested or reasonably verified using any working form of the scientific method.[52] Therefore, there remains the potential involvement of much empirically groundless speculation in the name of Scripture that is possibly spawned from sources other than the biblical texts—and perhaps even contrary to the texts themselves.[53]

Does this mean that if each of the proposed global Flood mechanisms were to be *successfully* refuted, orthodox-evangelical Christianity must finally concede that a global Flood makes no realistic empirical sense? We do not believe that to be the case at all. Having said that, it must first be averred that, whether or not one agrees or disagrees with the basic

---

52. In contrast to these models, see Wonderly, *God's Time-Records in Ancient Sediments*, 59–61. He presents a well-balanced conclusion drawn from current empirical conditions: "Actually, when we look at the processes which are going on today in nature, and include such catastrophic events as have occurred within human history, we have an adequate explanation for practically all that we see in the geologic record. Even though the great majority of the sedimentary strata are of such a nature that they could not have been formed by one or even several floods, the Biblical Flood probably could have been responsible for numerous alluvial deposits which are close to the surface, major changes in climate, and the onset of the most recent period of glaciation. Almost certainly involved in the Flood were a rapid change in sea level, and some movements in the earth's crust, with consequent elevation or lowering of certain geographic areas. These are illustrative of types of actions which could be produced during such a catastrophe as the Flood seems to have been. . . . It is reasonable to accept certain large destructive actions as having been produced by the Flood, but we should also recognize the thick deposits which are of an entirely different nature as having resulted from the slow processes which are still producing those kinds of deposits today" (60). This is a very empirically plausible position.

53. For instance, does a sound interpretation of the scriptural text require that the entire crust of the Earth (and possibly even the mantle as well) be completely transformed by the Noahic Flood? In fact, taking it back even deeper into chronological time, does a sound interpretation of the scriptural text require a young Earth? The answer one gives to the second question can drastically alter the answer one gives to the first question. For further on this subject, see *The Genesis Column*, 37–39.

conclusions of any or all of these Flood models, we must be careful not to make a blanket disavowal of all of their postulations. Sometimes, despite a wider system or model failure, particular aspects of that system or model can still ring true and be pertinent to a legitimate understanding of reality. It is wise to resist in our thinking an all-or-nothing mentality. A willingness to think with an open-mind and an integrationist view are essential in the earnest seeking of truth.

Moreover, it may be very possible for evidence of a global Flood to exist in the natural record despite the lack of a viable natural explanation for the causative mechanism of the Deluge itself. Therefore, as mentioned earlier, we will not focus primarily on mechanistic secondary causation, but rather on what the Flood may have left behind regardless of any natural mechanism that God may have used to carry out his divine global judgment of the Earth and its inhabitants.

THE POSSIBLE TRACE EVIDENCE

The key question that must be addressed is this: What does the evidence of nature really show in its plain, visible condition? There are a number of phenomena in the natural order that might reasonably be interpreted as extant trace evidence of a global Noahic Flood. Several of these will be presented and discussed. First, though, we need to make a bit of a disclaimer.

There are a few geological phenomena that are often mentioned as being Flood evidences, which however—from our Old-Earth perspective—must be either dismissed as such, or specially qualified. These occurrences include such things as turbidites,[54] megabreccias,[55] polystrate trees,[56] and fossil forests.[57]

Each of these phenomena are indeed real events of the natural order that are typically related to catastrophism. Hence, they are frequently used by advocates of YEC Flood Geology to accentuate what they perceive as being part and parcel with the catastrophic procession of the Earth during the time of the Noahic deluge. Since the typical YEC Flood view interprets the entire Phanerozoic sequence of the geologic column to be the diluvial consequence, it is easy and quite convenient to group all lithographic and paleontological phenomena—particularly those of a catastrophism nature—together as one big stirred-up-together batch of Flood evidence (think of a bucket of miscellaneous ingredients thoroughly mixed up and then poured and settled back out). With this viewpoint, there are no matters of deep time and uniformitarian processes of which to be seriously concerned. In fact, from the view of Flood Geology, there are really no significant matters of geochronological event placement at all. Everything in the crust of the Earth from, at least, the upper Precambrian basement rock to the lower Holocene strata are simply understood to be the current version of the jumbled up remains of the old antediluvian world. Therefore, in this line of thought,

---

54. See Bates and Jackson, "turbidite" and "turbidity current," in *Dictionary of Geological Terms*, 540: *turbidite*—"A sediment deposited from a turbidity current" / *turbidity current*—"A bottom-flowing current laden with suspended sediment, moving swiftly down a subaqueous slope and spreading horizontally on the floor of the body of water, having been set in motion by locally stirred-up sediment that gives the water a density greater than that of the surrounding clear water. Such currents are known to occur [even] in lakes, and are believed to have produced the submarine canyons notching the continental slope." It should also be noted that turbidity currents have also been known to transport very large rocks (clasts) from over a meter to five meters in diameter. For further, see Chadwick, "Megabreccias: Evidence for Catastrophism," 39–46.

55. Bates and Jackson, "breccia" and "megabreccia," in *Dictionary of Geological Terms*, 65, 317: *breccia*—"A coarse-grained clastic rock, composed of angular broken rock fragments held together by a mineral cement or a fine-grained matrix" (65) / *megabreccia*—[very large and extensive breccias] "A rock produced by collapse owing to salt solution, containing blocks that are randomly oriented and invariably inclined at angles from 6° to 25° and that range from a meter to more than 100m [328 ft.] in horizontal dimension [and] as much as 400m long [1,312 ft.], developed downslope from large thrusts by gravitational sliding. It is partly tectonic and partly sedimentary in origin, containing rocks that are shattered but little rotated" (317).

56. A *polystrate* is simply a fossil (most often a tree) that is encased within multiple (poly) layers of rock deposition (strata). The term was probably first coined by N. A. Rupke in 1966. For further, see Rupke, "Prolegomena to a Study of Cataclysmal Sedimentation," 152–57.

57. Fossil forests exist on every continent, including Antarctica.

The Evidence of Nature

though the faunal order in the strata is explained as being ecological zonation, it really does not matter where something is found because it is all just part of the comprehensive diluvial mix. In a word, Flood Geology places all of the Earth's geologic eggs—that is, those from the Cambrian Period to the time of Noah in the Quaternary Period—in the very same giant rock basket.

The problem with this notion is brought into plain view when the worldwide geologic record is seen both from a classic uniformitarian standpoint and in light of our Old-Earth Flood model. From this perspective, the above phenomena—turbidites, megabreccias, polystrate fossils, and fossil forests—are only pertinent to the Noahic Flood if they are shown to be related to our very specific geochronological timeline. In other words, in our model, these events could possibly be relevant to the Flood only if they occurred in the general time vicinity just immediately prior to 1.81 Ma, which is the proximate time when we posit the Noahic Flood to have happened. The reason why this is crucial is that catastrophic actions like turbidity currents and megabreccias are events that have transpired throughout large portions of the Earth's geologic history—including their occurrence throughout modern times (post-Flood) and, in fact, their ongoing occurrence still today. They are not in any way exclusive to the Flood of Noah.

Moreover, polystrate fossils (particularly polystrate trees) and fossil forests can occur by catastrophic events other than that of diluvial actions. Note, further, that it is also possible for them to be the result of local or regional (and not necessarily global) catastrophes. In fact, this is indeed typically the case. The mere existence of polystrate trees and fossil forests does not immediately associate them with the Noahic Flood. While we do concur that these incidents are evidence of some form of cataclysmal deposition, they can come about as the result of a number of different causes: a flood, a volcanic eruption, a glacial phenomenon, an impact, or some other type of catastrophe (or a combination of catastrophes). Therefore, for at least the reasons aforementioned, these particular forms of catastrophic events will *not* be considered to be general evidences in support of a global Flood. However, the last two—i.e., some *specific* polystrate trees as well as a *specific* fossil forest—shall be later entered into the conversation.

Now, we will discuss certain extant trace evidences that we believe can possibly point to a global Flood in our Old-Earth paradigm. These evidences will include the following: the epicontinental seas, the expansive sedimentation, the lay of the land, the mountaintop fossils, the deep water in the Earth, the Flood fit at the former Pliocene-Pleistocene boundary, and certain ancient plants that are still alive.

The Epicontinental Seas

An epicontinental (epeiric) sea, also known as an *inland sea*, is a large (usually) shallow body of predominantly salt water standing on a continental shelf or within a continent.[58] Epicontinental seas are characterized by having no direct connection to an ocean; they are essentially basin receptacles constantly kept filled by streams and by water runoff. Epeiric seas have existed worldwide throughout the continental history of the Earth. They are typically the result of the progression and recession of water (by flooding, ocean-level fluctuation, etc.) often combined with glacial action. Geologists believe that the basins of many inland seas are giant scars and depressions existing since very early land formation or later left behind by the retreat of heavy ice sheets. Examples of primeval epeiric seas that are no longer extant include the Zechstein Sea (central Europe: middle to late Permian Period),[59] the Sundance Sea (southwest Canada and Western United States: Jurassic Period),[60] the Western Interior Seaway (i.e., Niobraran Sea, which divided North America into sections: middle to late Cretaceous Period),[61] the Turgai Sea (Western Siberia from north of the present day Caspian Sea to the paleo-Arctic: mid-Jurassic Period to Oligocene Epoch),[62] the Tyrrell Sea (northeastern Canada: late Pleistocene Epoch to early Holocene Epoch),[63]

---

58. Bates and Jackson, "Epicontinental Sea," 167. See also, Howell, *Glossary of Geology*, 262: *Shallow inland seas*—"Seas in restricted communication with the open ocean having depths less than 250 meters. They may be looked upon as flooded continental areas. Hudson Bay is an example. Also known as Epeiric seas."

59. Smith, "Rapid marine transgressions and regressions of the Upper Permian Zechstein Sea," 155–56.

60. Kilibarda and Loope, "Jurassic aeolian oolite on a paleohigh in the Sundance Sea," 391–404.

61. Hampson, "Sediment Dispersal across Late Cretaceous Shelf," 1–21.

62. Enghof, "Historical Biogeography of the Holarctic," 223–63.

63. Lajeunesse and Allard, "The Nastapoka drift belt, eastern Hudson Bay," 65–76. The Tyrrell Sea was essentially the primeval version of the Hudson Bay (as it existed during the final recession phase of the Laurentide Ice Sheet). This current body of water is grounded in a structural basin that dates back to, at least, the late Ordovician Period. Therefore—as are the elemental basins of many epicontinental seas—its foundational existence is prehistoric and thus greatly predates anything possibly related to the Noahic Flood or the Pleistocene Ice Age. However, we are talking here about the basin itself and not the sea; basins are not always seas. They are subject to ongoing change. There are many factors that can result in such change, including, in this particular case, glaciation. Please note that glacial ice carries tremendous weight. This ground weight results in the downward movement of the Earth's crust (isostatic depression). Later, as the ice begins to melt/retreat and the ground weight is relieved, there is a crustal rebound effect (isostatic

and the Champlain Sea (Quebec-Ontario and New York-Vermont areas: late Pleistocene Epoch to early Holocene Epoch).[64] Know that the basins become seas when they are filled with water. Thus, these time demarcations (above) are indicators of when they were most recently filled with water. When they are no longer bodies of water, they are no longer seas. Two of the above former seas (one still extant, but in a different form)—the Tyrrell Sea and the Champlain Sea—due to their connection to the Ice age, will be mentioned in a later section.

There are presently existing epicontinental seas, including the Caspian Sea (bordered by Azerbaijan, Iran, Kazakhstan, Russia, and Turkmenistan: the largest true inland body of water in the world) and the Aral Sea (Uzbekistan and Kazakhstan: now only a "pond" of its former self).[65] Additionally, there are other bodies of water, such as the North Sea, the Persian Gulf, and the Hudson Bay (i.e., the relict of the Tyrrell Sea), that exist within a continent, yet have a direct connection to an external oceanic water source. There are still other significant bodies of water, such as the Black Sea (connected to the Aegean Sea by the Strait of Bosporus) and the Mediterranean Sea (connected to the Atlantic Ocean by the Strait of Gibraltar), that do not completely exist within a landmass, yet have only very narrow external oceanic water sources. These are not true epicontinental seas, although they are sometimes referred to as *marginal* epicontinental seas (because they are mostly enclosed by land).

While all oceans, seas, lakes, and other such wide bodies of water are in some form of continuous change, an epeiric sea has an extreme susceptibility to shoreline and depth modification due to its closed and restricted system.[66]

---

uplift). Both pre-glacial basins and glacial-induced bodies of water can be greatly affected by the isostatic movement. The Tyrrell Sea/Hudson Bay is a prime example of this; the Tyrrell Sea was a much larger body of water than is its present Hudson Bay relict. For a time, the Tyrrell Sea would have benefited both from the isostatic depressive effects (which lowered the basin) and from the immediate glacial melt effects. In this glacial-to-nonglacial transition, the ice melt would have likely occurred faster than the isostatic rebound adding significant water influx. However, this benefit was not permanent; for as the Laurentide glaciation retreated, the isostatic uplift gradually raised the basin back to its former depth and thus decreased the size of the sea. However, in this case (and unlike its Champlain Sea cousin), the Tyrrell basin has since remained, but just with a different name.

64. Clark and Karrow, "Late Pleistocene water bodies in the St. Lawrence Lowland, New York," 805–13. Similar to the Tyrrell Sea, the Champlain Sea was the result of glacial recession during the final phase of the Ice Age.

65. Roll et al., "Aral Sea," 1–21.

66. Ager, *The New Catastrophism*, 79–92.

An example of this phenomenon is the recent degradation of the Aral Sea. Due to a number of variant changes, including river water diversion, the Aral Sea—once the fourth largest inland body of water in the world—has lost ninety percent of its water volume over the last several decades (between 1960 and 2003).[67] It is in danger of drying up. The recent demise of the Aral has caused an ecological disaster in the region. True epicontinental seas can be extremely susceptible to changing conditions.

Epeiric seas have come and gone throughout natural history depending largely on the incoming volume from hydrological influents related to marine (oceans), fluvial (streams/rivers), pluvial (rainfall), diluvial (floods), and glacial (ice/meltwater) events, etc. This same dynamic is also true of the largest "inland" seas, such as the Black Sea and the Mediterranean Sea, even though they are not true epicontinental seas.[68] One has only to troll across the continents of the Earth to see the conspicuous dry remains of ancient shorelines that are now deserts and modern shorelines that were once deserts. This sternly refutes the common presumption that seas and coastlines have remained the same for eons.[69] When it comes to epeiric seas, in particular, significant change is understood to be much more of a rule than an exception. And like giant terrestrial mud puddles left behind after a raging and torrential tempest—or after the melting and retreat of the drifts

---

67. Roll et al., "Aral Sea," 1–21, esp. 5–6.

68. See Ryan and Pitman, *Noah's Flood: The New Scientific Discoveries*. Ryan and Pitman present interesting data showing a possible very ancient flooding event (they date it at 5–7 Ma) of the "Mediterranean Desert" through "Gibraltar's Waterfall" (73–92). They say: "The Gibraltar dam must have collapsed catastrophically. Salt water from the "bathyal realm" of the Atlantic had inundated the Mediterranean desert at the pace of thousands of Niagara Falls. In the process the raging torrents had eroded the former barrier, incising the breach to perhaps one thousand feet below the level of the inrushing Atlantic. . . . Although no humans lived five million years ago, had any been present, they would have witnessed the Mediterranean desert disappearing permanently beneath a mile of salt water in a matter of a single human lifetime (92). However, they also conclude that another more recent event (c. 5,600 B.C.) whereby the salt water of the Aegean Sea arm of the Mediterranean Sea burst through the "Bosporus Dam" and catastrophically flooded the fresh water of the Black Sea basin, i.e., the New Euxine Freshwater Lake (which at the time was significantly below sea-level and very different than it is today). This flood devastated a great human civilization located in the area. They suggest that this regional flood event might very well be the phenomenon from which the biblical myth of Noah's Flood was derived. Ryan and Pitman even posit that this event led to massive human migrations away from the area and into present day Europe (188–201). Of course, just to be clear, we do not hold that either of these flood events—even if they did indeed occur as posited—are the Noahic Flood. They do not fit the biblical parameters.

69. Ager, *The New Catastrophism*, 81–82.

of Winter snow and ice, perhaps some of these seas are the persevering, yet ever-fleeting relicts of things from the past much greater than themselves.

The Expansive Sedimentation

Sedimentation exists on all the continents of the Earth. It is found on ocean floors and even on mountaintops.[70] The process of sedimentation[71] is always occurring, but sediments[72]—the product of sedimentation—are not always remaining. Ager appropriately differentiates between two types of sedimentation:

> [I]t is important to distinguish between ephemeral sedimentation that comes and goes with the seasons and permanent sedimentation that actually accumulates and stays. My main complaint concerning students of modern sediments is that they pay more attention to the question of how sediments are deposited than to the question as to whether or not they stay there. . . . Even when sediment is recorded, it is frequently in the form of sand waves that move from place to place and do not accumulate.[73]

Therefore, Ager emphasizes the difference between temporary deposition (viz., particles in continuous transience—"comes and goes") and permanent accumulation (viz., particles becoming a rock layer—"actually . . . stays"). He adds a significant comment:

> Most of the sediment in fact seems to be accumulating close inshore and very little gets to the outer shelf or the deeps. It has been calculated that there has been an average of about 9m of deposition close inshore during the last 5000 years. Coupled with this, however, we have to remember the huge concentration of such sediment in deltas such as that of the Mississippi, where it has

---

70. Ross, *The Genesis Question*, 158.

71. See Bates and Jackson, *Dictionary of Geological Terms*, 454. Sedimentation is "The process of forming sediment in layers, including the separation of rock particles from the parent material, the transportation of these particles to the site of deposition, the actual deposition or settling, the diagenetic changes occurring in the sediment, and its ultimate consolidation into rock."

72. Bates and Jackson, *Dictionary of Geological Terms*, 453. Sediment is "solid fragmental material transported and deposited by wind, water, or ice, chemically precipitated from solution, or secreted by organisms, and that forms in layers in loose unconsolidated form, e.g. sand, mud, till."

73. Ager, *The Nature of the Stratigraphical Record*, 73–74.

been accumulating at a fantastic rate (perhaps 3000m in the same period of time).[74]

This means that sedimentary accumulation of a lasting nature typically occurs at a higher rate "close inshore" (i.e., near the land, but still in the sea) than it does at any other locale (including the outer continental shelf, the deep ocean, and especially on land). In fact, very little vertical accumulation typically occurs on the dry epicontinent.[75] Most sedimentation on the continental land areas is more lateral (often wind-blown from place to place) than vertical and thus is somewhat transitory. Just a few feet of epicontinental strata could be the result of many millions of years of sedimentary deposition. This means that there are (and should be) gaps in the sedimentary rock record (both subaerial and subaqueous), but especially subaerial. As Ager says:

> Sedimentation goes on all the time, for ever moving from place to place, for ever cannibalizing itself. Subsidence [i.e., the downward settling of the Earth's surface]—on the scale we are concerned with here—is generally a quite different matter and must be involved with the internal processes of the earth. It is only when sedimentation and subsidence coincide that the conditions will be right for the preservation of the vast thicknesses that constitute the stratigraphical record.[76]

Both the "vast thicknesses" and the gaps tell the story of natural history.[77] Cvancara says that "any place on Earth preserves only the vestige of a complete rock record or geologic time."[78] Similar to Ager's net image, Moshier

---

74. Ager, *The Nature of the Stratigraphical Record*, 74.

75. Ager, *The Nature of the Stratigraphical Record*, 52–53. Ager remarks: "I maintain that a far more accurate picture of the stratigraphical record is of one long gap with only occasional sedimentation.... Perhaps the best way to convey this attitude is to remember a child's definition of a net as a lot of holes tied together with string. The stratigraphical record is a lot of holes tied together with sediment. It is though one has a newspaper delivered only for the football results on Saturdays and assumes that nothing at all happened on the other days of the week.... No doubt my prejudices are coloured by having looked at too much epicontinental sediment and not enough oceanic, but I must plead in my defense that this is the nature of the stratigraphical record on the continents anyway."

76. Ager, *The Nature of the Stratigraphical Record*, 95.

77. Ager, *The Nature of the Stratigraphical Record*, 53. Ager states: "[T]he sedimentary pile at any one place on the earth's surface is nothing more than a tiny and fragmentary record of vast periods of earth history. This may be called the 'Phenomenon of the Gap Being More Important than the Record.'" While his point is well taken, we suggest that the gap and the preserved strata are equally important and that the gap is also part of the record.

78. Cvancara, *A Field Manual for the Amateur Geologist*, 122.

The Evidence of Nature

and Hill appropriately liken the gaps to "pages or whole chapters ripped out of the binding of the [Earth geological history] book."[79] Note that these gaps (or unconformities) do not negate any reality of passed time, but only the physical record of that time at that particular location. Yet, even the gaps in the record at one location can be filled in from a more complete record at other locations.[80] While all of the copies of Earth's "book" of geologic history are extremely antiquated and are heavily worn from the passage of deep time, not every copy has the very same pages "ripped out." But—pages are frequently missing from each of the copies. This phenomenon is an expectation of basic geology.

In the case of the Noahic Flood, it seems to be very plausible to conclude that there may not be a visibly significant and permanent Noahic sedimentary stratum in the column. The Flood event, in the context of deep time, was *very* short in duration (approximately only one year long). This short window just would not provide enough time for the event itself to generate the amount of heavy sediment necessary to survive unto permanent global stratification. Due to this lack of heavy sediment laid down and also considering (again, in the context of deep time) that the event occurred somewhat recently (immediately prior to 1.81 Ma in our paradigm), the deposition that was initially generated across the Earth became largely cannibalized prior to having the time to uniformly lithify. Following Ager, for permanent stratification to occur, both the external and internal processes of the Earth must collaborate very carefully in sedimentary production, preservation, and compacting subsidence. Such an across-the-board collaboration does not happen everywhere every day—or even every megaannum. This is precisely why the gaps in the strata must also be considered part of the stratigraphic record. It is also why the absence of permanent and widespread strata does not in itself negate the reality of an event.

Furthermore, in consideration of the above and in line with the reckonings of basic geology, any extant elements of Noahic sediments should be widely distributed, yet very fragmented ("gappy"), very pocketed, and quite frankly, very hard to discern. Nonetheless, there is much unlithified and interspersed alluvial sediment[81] (as well as some that is lithified) extensively

---

79. Moshier and Hill, "Missing Time Gaps in the Rock Record," 99.

80. See Stallings, *The Genesis Column*, 46–48.

81. *Alluvium* is loose sediment that can be of a sorted or unsorted nature, and made up of such things as clay, silt, sand, mud, and various forms of gravel that were distributed and deposited by water action.

found in the vicinity of the Calabrian-Gelasian boundary.[82] This includes sweeping marine fossils (e.g., macrofossils, foraminifera, calcareous nannofossils, diatomaceous material, etc.) and other flood compatible formations and debris.[83]

Interestingly, a recent study (2017) by Tim Clarey shows the existence of a definitive carbonate deposition in the geologic column from near the K-T boundary and upward into the Miocene-Pliocene sequence.[84] This is significant because carbonate rock is formed underwater. According to the study, this carbonate presence runs across large portions of the Earth, including that of North Africa, the Middle East, and Europe.[85] This data is actually supportive of Wonderly's assertion that "the Biblical Flood probably could have been responsible for numerous alluvial deposits which are close to the surface."[86] While Clarey is a YEC geologist and is understandably presenting his data from a stratigraphic ecological zonation perspective (rather than a standard uniformitarian view), it is particularly intriguing that the carbonate deposition, although beginning in the lower Tertiary strata, runs right up to the relative geochronological point of the Noahic Flood demarcation in our OEC postulation (that is, into the Pliocene rocks of the upper Tertiary and right up to the lower Quaternary system). Thus, as related to extant marine sedimentation, the main point is this: There is wide-ranging carbonate trace evidence in the upper Tertiary stratigraphy (i.e., the layers of the Pliocene Epoch; approaching the rock record of the Pleistocene "Ice Age" Epoch). Again, while there is much imprecision here, this general carbonate "clearing up" boundary is still the general *proximate point* where we locate the Noahic Flood in our OEC time-line.

Furthermore, it is also probable that there are sedimentary remains from the Flood which exist but are not clearly discernable as such in the mix. Young makes this comment:

---

82. See Macri et al., "Magnetic Fabric of Plio-Pleistocene sediments from Crotone fore-arc basin," 67–79; cf. Calvo et al., "Alternating diatomaceous and volcanistic deposits in Milo Island, Greece," 24–40; Scheiderich et al., "Molybdenum isotope, multiple sulfur isotope, and redox-sensitive element behavior in early Pleistocene Mediterranean sapropels," 134–44. Note that *sapropels* are rich, dark, organic marine sediments.

83. As should be expected, there are also glacial compatible markers here as well.

84. Clarey, "Local Catastrophes or Receding Floodwater?," 100–20. Please do not confuse this particular deposition with the much lower and earlier Carboniferous-Permian strata, which is related to hyper atmospheric oxygenation and correspondent massive plant life profusion and subsequent laying down.

85. Clarey, "Local Catastrophes or Receding Floodwater?," 100–20.

86. Wonderly, *God's Time-Records*, 60.

There is also the very strong possibility that a great flood could have produced rather ephemeral kinds of geologic deposits. One might expect the development of widespread silt and gravel deposits and piles of debris that could well be eroded away quickly. It is entirely possible that the Genesis flood may have in some fashion covered much of the globe's surface and produced a great redistribution of materials. Since that time much of the physical evidence for such a flood could easily have been destroyed or rendered difficult to decipher. Remnants of flood deposits scattered around the world would be extremely difficult to correlate stratigraphically or geochronologically.[87]

We affirm this thinking. Unlike the view of Whitcomb and Morris and their ilk, it is not a necessity to attribute *all* permanent strata above the Precambrian-Cambrian boundary, or even *any* permanent strata at all, to the Noahic Flood.[88] And unlike the view of Ross and his ilk, any absence of a clear-cut Noahic sedimentary layer does not negate the Flood's global occurrence.[89] Both, we believe, are unnecessary extremes. After all, in addition to the carbonate deposition, there are plenty of other Quaternary sedimentary alluvial deposits across the face of the Earth that very well may be Noahic related, yet not clearly stratified and identifiable as such.[90] When it comes to stratigraphy, absence of evidence is not always evidence of absence: remember, gaps can also be evidence of presence no longer visible.

Additionally, any stratification of sediments would more likely occur significantly post-Flood after the water settled into its permanent basins and entered into processes of long-term diagenesis (i.e., through hydrothermal action, compaction, cementation, etc.). Some sediments would probably even enter into metamorphics (i.e., those sediments that found their way deeper into the column and encountered massive internal heat and pressure) and thus become changed. Moreover, due to the nature of such a cataclysm, many overtly Flood-related sediments were likely transported recessionally from the continents into the post-Flood oceans and eventually subducted into the continental margins. This, quite candidly, may very well explain why

---

87. Young, *Creation and the Flood*, 174.

88. Wonderly, *God's Time Records*, 60.

89. Ross, *The Genesis Question*, 154, 158–59. Ross attributes the presence of sedimentary layers (and marine fossils on mountains) primarily to plate tectonics.

90. See J. Lawrence Kulp, "Deluge Geology," 1–15. Here he states that "it is important for the Christian geologist to carefully study the truly superficial erosional and depositional effects on the earth to obtain evidence on the extent and nature of the flood of Noah" (15). Again, also read Wonderly, *God's Time-Records*, 59–61.

the carbonate deposition mentioned in the Clarey report can be found as far down in the geologic column as the Cretaceous-Tertiary boundary.[91]

Despite the above postulations, there remains a common belief among many people that a global Flood scenario of Noahic duration (roughly a year) should leave behind to this present day a very clearly discernable sedimentary deposit, with definable erosional surfaces, and significant topographical/geographical modifications. However, a recent study (2018) by Moshier, who is a geologist at Wheaton College, seems to show evidence to the contrary. While Moshier is not an advocate of a global Flood, in the interest of research, he decided to apply what science knows about tsunamis—which are the most catastrophic observable local diluvial events presently operating in nature—and "scale up" everything to a much greater level in order to simulate probable global Flood geological effects.[92] Tsunamis are characterized by rapid rising water which can often traverse very long distances with great force and incredible impact. According to Moshier, a tsunami wave can easily move toward land at 10-20 miles per hour for several kilometers at a height of up to thirty meters above normal sea-level. Such a massive demonstration of power can devastate virtually all manmade structures in its path.[93] However, what typical effect does such an awesome event have on natural geological formations? According to Moshier, not really that much:

> [G]eologists have discovered that tsunami sediment deposits are generally less than 25 centimeters (10 inches) thick and conform to the antecedent landscape (that is, no significant change in topography). Large coastal storms also surge water landward of the coast, but storm deposits are only slightly thicker and confined to the beach near the shore."[94]

In other words, tsunamis do not significantly change the greater sedimentary deposition or greatly modify the basic topographical landscape of a targeted geographic area. Essentially, any new sedimentary deposits would be thin, transient, and temporary, and would be generally conformed to the previous landforms. So, how would this specific work be applied to a worldwide flood?

First, there would be a diluvial inundation phase:

---

91. See the forthcoming section in this chapter, "The Deep Water in the Earth." It is very possible that the post-Flood transfer of water into the deep recesses of the Earth also involved the leaching of significant sediments and chemicals, including carbonates.

92. Moshier, "Geology does not Support a Worldwide Flood," 159.

93. Moshier, "Geology does not Support a Worldwide Flood," 159.

94. Moshier, "Geology does not Support a Worldwide Flood," 159.

We estimated that to flood the earth to the highest mountains in 150 days would require water to rise just over 100 feet per day (and fall at about that same rate). While this sounds like a dramatic rise, especially to any living soul not in the ark, it's possible that not all that much sediment would be produced or moved very far during the advance or fall. Most of the geological work of erosion would occur at the water-land interface (the rising shoreline), but just as with a surging tsunami there is not much time to excavate large quantities of sediment. Furthermore, at 10 miles per hour for a typical tsunami (which equals 126,720 feet per day), that's some 1,130 times faster than our estimate for the rising or falling of global floodwater! A rate of 100 feet per day is far too slow to move even grains of sand![95]

Second, there would be a diluvial recession phase of about the same time duration: "During the 150-day period of water recession, more sediment may be eroded and transported to lower elevations, but again, the velocity of the receding floodwater is not too effective to erode or move sediment."[96] Although there can also be other forces involved in the processes during the inundation and recession phases, the Moshier study shows that there would likely not be any overt amounts of sediment available to be moved and redistributed.

The fair and honest conclusion is that even something so all-encompassing as a year-long global Flood event—indeed, even one initiated by tsunami-type forces—would not be capable of producing the massive and devastating topographical and stratigraphic modifications to the Earth as suggested by YEC, nor would it leave remarkable amounts of *permanent* alluvial sediments—that is, no definitive stratigraphic boundary—throughout the entire geologic record. In fact, Moshier's postulation actually seems to be subtly—and scripturally—confirmed by the enduring pre- *and* post-Flood presence of such currently existing terrestrial phenomena as the Tigris and Euphrates rivers (see earlier section).[97]

---

95. Moshier, "Geology does not Support a Worldwide Flood," 159–60.

96. Moshier, "Geology does not Support a Worldwide Flood," 160.

97. While much is frequently made in many circles of the renowned Tigris and Euphrates rivers (Gen 2:14), it is also important to comment on the other two of the four rivers of the scriptural Eden (Gen 2:10–13): the oft-forgotten rivers Pishon and Gihon—both, of which, may still remain. The Pishon River could very well be an ancient form of the Nile River, which obviously still exists. Talmudic scholar, Rabbi Rashi (Shlomoh ben Yitzchak), believed this to be the case (*Bereishis*, 25). However, 1st century historian, Josephus, associated the Pishon with the Ganges River and the Gihon with the Nile (*Antiquities* 1.1.3). Further, though some objectors would assert that there are problems with

The Genesis Cataclysm

As a reminder, there is also very little concerning ephemeral sedimentation (unconsolidated/unstratified/unlithified) that is overtly neat and clear-cut, even under normal conditions. This reality of obscureness would surely be magnified during the recessional processes of a global Flood event. Moreover, both the ongoing external (wind, rain, currents, etc.) and internal forces (tectonics, subduction, orogenesis, etc.) of the Earth—both in the immediate time period of the diluvial aftermath as well as in the ages since—continue to modify the visible look and placement of sediments and other detritus. This would make Noahic sediments, regardless of how expansive, very difficult to

---

his view in relation to the current geographical layout, Edward Ullendorff has argued that the Gihon is actually the Abbay River in Ethiopia, which is also known as the Blue Nile—and which also still exists (*Ethiopia and the Bible*, 2, 5). Note that this has long since been a *very strong* belief among the Ethiopian people. There have, of course, been other suggested identifications as well for both of these primeval rivers. While each of these views have, perhaps, some degree of merit, we take somewhat of a conciliatory approach to the matter. Though certainly no one knows for sure, please consider this possibility: If the present-day Red Sea were to be thought of as a post-Flood (marginal epeiric sea) relict (and thus not a *sea* in the antediluvian world), then the rift valley which encapsulates the Nile River (in Africa) along with the rift valley which encapsulates the Jordan River (in Jordan, Palestine, and Israel), could easily be the remaining features that once connected the very heart of Ethiopia (and, indeed, the heart of the entire African sub-continent) with Mesopotamia and the ancient Fertile Crescent. The Great Syro-African Depression (of which the Jordan Rift Valley is of the northernmost portion and the Nile Rift Valley is part of the central to southern portion) runs from Lebanon in the north through Lake Hula all the way down through the Dead Sea, the Aqaba, the Red Sea region, and as far south into Africa as Mozambique. Its total length is essentially a direct north-south run of approximately 3,700 miles. Moreover, the biblical record does, in fact, assert that the Gihon once ran just west of Old Jerusalem (called "the city of David"; cf. 2 Chr 32:30, 33:14—and, by the way, this was in *post*-Flood times). Therefore, when viewing the geo-topography of the greater multi-continental region, it is not hard at all to imagine the antediluvian version of the Gihon flowing southward past the place later to be occupied by the City of David and being then connected to the Blue Nile in Ethiopia. In this light, it seems very reasonable then to believe that the Nile may indeed be the modern rendition of the Pishon (following Rashi) and, likewise, the Blue Nile may be the current progeny of the Gihon (following Ullendorff)—both cut off from their original Mesopotamian sources after the Noahic Flood. Be aware that these great rift valleys—which are actually tectonic depressions related to continental plate collision pressure—would not have been, in our understanding, grossly affected by the Flood and thus would have remained intact (post-Flood). The changing of the river patterns in that very low altitude (particularly in the southernmost part of the Jordan Rift Valley, which is the very lowest point on Earth) could have easily been the result of ephemeral modification during Flood recession and still later effected by other area environmental factors (possibly as related to a Dead Sea area transform fault and the degradation of water sources). Therefore, it is a plausible possibility that the Jordan River is also a relict of the Pishon, whereas along with the Gihon, the two channels once ran somewhat parallel downward out of the upper Tigris-Euphrates network into Africa, but are today broken up.

currently identify in the general mix. Even with paleosol (fossil soil)[98] studies (note that paleosols are found on all continents and are often connected with alluvial deposition), there is no way to be absolutely certain in this particular regard. Therefore, it is our contention that while there are many pockets of extant alluvial deposition in the geologic column at various regions of our suggested Flood placement point, no significant permanent sedimentary stratification should be expected. In fact, in terms of sedimentation and surficial detritus, we strongly suggest that in the present 1.81 Ma—give-or-take a millennium or so—aftermath of a global Flood of an approximate one-year duration, what we see in the world today is pretty much what we should envisage seeing in the world today.

The Lay of the Land

As to the basic physical topography of the Earth, what is it that we find? Across the terrestrial sphere, from the peaks to the valleys, certainly the numerous features are varied. Yet, in the midst of all the planetary variety, there remains an ongoing commonality that should not be missed.

There are many continental plains,[99] peneplains,[100] bajadas,[101] pediments,[102] and pediplains (multiple pediments), etc. around the world,

---

98. A *paleosol* is an old—sometimes very ancient—deposit of soil (i.e., "fossil soil"; sometimes it is even called a "former soil") that is either embedded/entrapped within, underneath, or between sequences of sedimentary deposition and/or sequences of volcanic deposition.

99. Bates and Jackson, *Dictionary of Geological Terms*, 387. A *plain* is "Any flat area, large or small, at a low elevation; an extensive region of level or gently undulating land."

100. Bates and Jackson, *Dictionary of Geological Terms*, 375. A *peneplain* is "A low, nearly featureless, gently undulating land surface of considerable area, which presumably has been produced by the processes of long-continued mass-wasting, sheetwash, and stream erosion almost to base level in the penultimate stage of a humid, fluvial geomorphic cycle."

101. Bates and Jackson, *Dictionary of Geological Terms*, 40. A *bajada* is "A broad, gently inclined detrital surface extending from the base of mountain ranges out into an inland basin, formed by the lateral coalescence of alluvial fans, and having an undulating character due to the convexities of the component fans. It occurs most commonly in semiarid and desert regions, as in the SW U.S."

102. Bates and Jackson, *Dictionary of Geological Terms*, 372–73. A *pediment* is "A broad gently sloping erosion surface or plain of low relief, typically developed by running water, in an arid or semiarid region at the base of an abrupt and receding mountain front; it is underlain by bedrock that may be bare but is more often mantled with a thin discontinuous veneer of alluvium derived from the upland masses and in transit across the surface."

including some that are very large. They are all a part of a cause and effect relationship with water. This is the basic global "lay of the land." While this is true everywhere, it is much more visible in certain locales. Nevin M. Fenneman asserts, for example, that the Great Plains of the Western United States (which run from the Rocky Mountains to the Central Lowlands) is "mainly flood plain."[103] Clark concurs: "The high plains of the United States, from Texas to Montana, appear to have been great flood plains, like alluvial fans."[104] He adds further:

> Every evidence indicates that great erosive forces carved the general contours of the bedrocks, after which vast volumes of water, overloaded with sediment, built up alluvial fans above the eroded surfaces. Conditions as we know them today would not produce these deposits. Violent water action is required to spread this gravel so widely and thickly.[105]

Similar conditions exist in India[106] and Bangladesh, particularly those of the Ganges River and Brahmaputra River floodplains; also, this is prominent in the Paris Basin of France, the Amazon River floodplain in Brazil, the Pantanal Floodplain in Brazil, Bolivia, and Paraguay, and other major plains located in Burma.[107] They are also found in southern Africa as well as in central and western Australia.[108] There are many other examples; these water-caused paleoplain formations are worldwide.[109]

In essence, the continents actually serve as drainage plains for water. This is systemic. Every stream on the planet is surrounded by some form of drainage basin.[110] Some basins are extremely expansive in size. For example, the Mississippi River basin encompasses over forty percent of the continental

---

103. Fenneman, *Physiography of Western United States*, 91. This book is part of Fenneman's classic two-volume set, which also includes, *Physiography of Eastern United States*.

104. Clark, *Genesis and Science*, 85–86.

105. Clark, *Genesis and Science*, 86.

106. Clark, *Genesis and Science*, 82.

107. Clark, *Genesis and Science*, 83–84.

108. Austin, "Did Landscapes Evolve?."

109. Baulig, "Peneplains and Pediplains," 913–30. He asserts that all current continental land surfaces are probably the result of ancient pediplanation followed by long-term erosive equilibrium.

110. Murck, *Geology*, 198.

The Evidence of Nature

United States.¹¹¹ Adjacent drainage areas are separated by *divides* that are of a higher elevation than the drainage basins. As Murck explains,

> On continents, great mountain chains separate streams that drain toward one side of the continent from streams that drain toward the other side. The continental divide of Western North America lies along the length of the Rocky Mountains. Streams to the east ultimately drain into the Atlantic Ocean, while those to the west drain into the Pacific Ocean.¹¹²

Since surface water is always seeking its own level, it constantly finds its way and moves toward its ultimate reservoir—the "world ocean."¹¹³ This is significant. According to Murck:

> Most of the water on our planet is contained in three huge interconnected basins—the Pacific, Atlantic, and Indian Oceans. (The Arctic Ocean is an extension of the Atlantic.) All three are connected with the Southern Ocean, the body of water that encircles Antarctica. Collectively, these four vast interconnected bodies of water, together with about 20 smaller seas, make up the "world ocean."¹¹⁴

This is an ongoing process that will continue as long as there is water and land. It is a system controlled by the basic law of gravity, the basic properties of water, the basic actions of erosion, and the basic geophysiography of the continental landmasses.¹¹⁵ Along with other terrestrial elements, running water and land significantly affect one another.¹¹⁶ Lambert makes this powerful comment:

---

111. Murck, *Geology*, 198.
112. Murck, *Geology*, 198.
113. Murck, *Geology*, 205.
114. Murck, *Geology*, 204–5.
  115. We also must remember that the continental landmass amalgamations have been in constant change, at least, since the first appearance of inhabitable land (Gondwana) at approximately 475 Ma (and probably even a bit before that—perhaps as early as 510 Ma). Since then, the continental landmasses have remained in an ongoing slow, but steady supercontinent cycle of formation, breakup, and dispersal in systematic repeats. In other words, what is present today is merely the most recent formation. For further, see *The Genesis Column*, 76–80.
  116. Note that this description is essentially akin to a basic contemporary (and less *idealized*) Davisian understanding of geomorphology, which is similarly uniformitarian with regards to geography as is the predominant view of mainstream science with regards to geology. In fact, within this neo-Davisian notion, both the geological and the physiographical forces of the planet are constantly active. In this sense, unlike with our

> Soon after land appears above the sea, rivers set about attacking it. Rivers rise in highlands and flow downhill to empty in a sea or inland drainage basin. The force of their moving water erodes and transports a load of soil and rock, so carving valleys that dissect mountains into peaks and ridges and reducing these to hills. But rivers also deposit the eroded debris to build lowland plains and offshore underwater platforms.[117]

While modern science tends to provide reasonable *local* descriptions for many of these ongoing events, such a focus makes it is quite easy to miss the bigger picture. The fact of the widespread intercontinental abundance of these local phenomena as well as the very fact of their composite existence is quite striking. The big question is "Why?" Why is the *physiographical system* of the Earth (with its universal planal format inundated with rivers, streams, and basins—all of which drain into the world ocean[118]) the way it is? To answer this question with complete authenticity, any and all naturalistic explanations must be understood within a supernaturalistic metaphysical framework. After all, God did create the Earth and all of the natural order. Though it is now currently in a fallen state, it is still God's property and he is still working in and through it to accomplish his purposes. This means that there is indeed a divinely designed land/water system in place that is quite vital and functionally purposeful. It has many moving parts with both

---

lunar neighbor, major internal processes such as geothermal operations, plate tectonics, and orogeny—along with the common external forces—are understood to be a modifying and recycling feature of the Earth's ongoing crustal system.

117. Lambert, *The Field Guide to Geology*, 116.

118. For an illustration, see Fenneman, *Physiography of Eastern United States*, 1–3. The continental "lay of the land" is strikingly systemic, particularly with regard to water. For example, regarding the southeastern margin of the United States, Fenneman presents an excellent description of the relationship between the *submerged* continental shelf and the *emerged* coastal plain: "The eastern and southern margin of the United States is a lowland which passes under the sea almost without change of its very gentle slope. The plain continues under shallow water for a distance varying from a few miles to a few hundred miles. Then the slope steepens and descends rapidly to the abyss. In studying the larger problems of the earth and its history this steep slope is taken to mark the edge of the continental mass. The plain under shallow water, generally less than 600 feet deep, is treated as part of the continent. It belongs there just as the Mississippi Valley does, both having been dry land and shallow sea repeatedly. Even now, throughout most of the coast, shallow sea is changing to lowland or the reverse is taking place" (1). While this is a specific example, please note that in a general sense, this description systemically fits the land/ocean relationship of continental masses all over the world. Geologically speaking, the coastal plain and the continental shelf are essentially the same thing. Each is simply defined and differentiated by the current presence or lack of presence of covering water.

internal and external features; yet, it is also a whole. Sometimes while we remain so zeroed on the narrow and the specific, we miss the system that encompasses all of the narrows and specifics. Moreover, in so doing, we not only miss the system through which God works, but we also miss grasping the place that the narrows and specifics have in that very purposeful system.

Apart from the benefit of the biblical revelation to see things from the greater meta-perspective, perhaps we have all developed the tendency to frequently view and interpret phenomena a bit too locally.[119] A good strong look at the intercontinental physiography from a "giant step back" can cause one to reasonably wonder whether, at some singular point in relatively "recent" natural history (say, within the last two million years),[120] water may have been simultaneously everywhere (short-term)[121]—just as it once was before (but, long-term) in the more distant past (i.e., from the Archaean Eon into the Ordovician Period).[122] Be reminded, again, that the ground on the Earth has been a water drainage plain since the advent of first land. Perhaps it deserves consideration that the current global "lay of the land" is to some

---

119. It is easy to unwittingly lose sight of the larger view. Just as a perspectival frame of reference, my family and I reside in Wilson, North Carolina, which is located in the ENC Coastal Plain. Our city and community do not in any way resemble "the beach." We are, in fact, a good 144 miles from Manteo, North Carolina, which, from our direction, is the primary gateway to NC's Outer Banks. (Comparatively, Wilson is 112 miles from Morehead City—NC's Crystal Coast; and 120 miles from Wilmington—NC's Southern Coast.) Much of the land between Wilson and Manteo consists of rural farming country replete with barns, livestock, tobacco and corn fields and easily provides a visual non-coastal illusion. However, the reality is that we are on the exact same geologic parcel as those places which are currently in direct contact with the waves of the Atlantic Ocean. It is *all* coastal plain. Sometimes it's good for us to periodically look up just to see and understand where we really are.

120. This is actually very recent if the Earth is 4.567 billion years old, which is what we posit to be the case. See Ogg et al., *The Concise Geologic Time Scale*, 23–24; cf. Stallings, *The Genesis Column*, 39–43.

121. For instance, see Fenneman, 6, 7, 10, 12, 31, and 44. Here he provides several very detailed and powerful topographical diagrams of certain large regions of the Western United States. His presentation of the Great Plains Province (see pages 1–91 for text) with its detailed web of streambeds, riverbeds, sand dunes, sandstone structure, and various plains causes one to see the moving and draining effects of water on the land in a very big way.

122. See Burnham and Berry, "Formation of Hadean granites by melting of igneous crust," 457–61. From a recent study of zircon mineral grains preserved in sandstone rocks, Burnham and Berry were able to construct a profile of the conditions of post-Hadean primeval Earth which confirms that the planet was at that time desolate and barren, without mountains, and almost completely covered by water. Of course, this postulation of a primeval "water world" is not a new notion within orthodox science.

degree a *subtle* recessional scar remaining from great worldwide oceans of the past, including the short-term Noahic Flood ocean and the consequentially successive post-Flood Ice Age effects—abrasions, erosions, moraines, etc.—combined with more recent modifications from ongoing uniform natural processes intermixed with periodic local and regional catastrophic events. In other words, what we observe today in the grossly water-effected earthen landscape is the ongoing aftermath of a divine meta-anomaly both preceded and postceded by relatively regular geomorphics. While we do not believe that the Noahic Flood completely changed the topography (and certainly not the deeper crust) of the Earth, when we look at things with both eyes open, the global "lay of the land" seems to be very compatible with global post-Flood images.

The Mountaintop Fossils

There are many types of fossils found on mountaintops, including fossils of a marine origin.[123] This obviously and undeniably implies a connection between a previous oceanic environment and the current alpine environment. Modern science typically explains this relationship in terms of plate tectonics and orogenic uplift.[124] For instance, according to Mark Isaak:

> Shells on mountains are easily explained by uplift of the land. Although this process is slow, it is observed happening today, and it accounts not only for the seashells on mountains but also for the other geological and paleontological features of those mountains. The sea once did cover the areas where the fossils are found, but they were not mountains at the time; they were shallow seas.[125]

Isaak also adds that a diluvial interpretation is not plausible because floods cause orogenic erosion which results in sedimentary deposition into the valleys.[126] His idea seems to be that the dynamics of a flood would not allow the hard remains of any marine creatures to remain on a place of high ground. The diluvial recession process would move the marine remains and other sedimentary debris to the lower points from the higher points. Additionally, he provides the common assertion that many of the

---

123. Coffin, "Famous Fossils from a Mountaintop," 45–47.
124. Browne, "Whale Fossils High in Andes Show How Mountains Rose from Sea."
125. Isaak, "Claim CC364: Marine fossils on mountains."
126. Isaak, "Claim CC364: Marine fossils on mountains."

mountaintop fossils are found *in situ* (pro orogenesis) and thus not in a state of redeposition (contra Flood).[127]

It is without a doubt, due to the nature of orogenesis, that many of the mountaintop marine fossils are where they are through diastrophism (crustal movement) as manifested in tectonic uplift.[128] Mountains do rise and fall. This process is observably occurring today. Mount Everest, for instance, has a current official elevation of 29,029 feet, which is actually twelve feet lower than it was in 1999.[129] Such phenomena are obviously measurable. When orogeny occurs, the crust of the Earth—along with the detritus contents of that crust—are moved upward. Likewise, in a flood recession, sediments and debris can and will be transferred as the water moves from the higher areas to the lower areas. However, there are two critical matters of consideration here. The first is whether or not orogenesis can satisfactorily account for *all* of the mountaintop fossils. The second is whether or not flood recession would completely cleanse *all* diluvial signs away from the high points to the low points. It seems reasonable that if the Noahic Flood were indeed a global event, there would probably still be some sort of flood debris present in unique places (including some hard fossil seashells on mountaintops). After all, the scriptural revelation does indeed assert that the waters of the Noahic Flood "prevailed so mightily upon the earth that all the high mountains under the whole heaven were covered" (Gen 7:19). These considerations are not intended to negate in any way the concept of orogenic uplift. However, since modern science posits that the continental landmasses were in their approximate current positions by the late Tertiary Period (although plate

---

127. Isaak, "Claim CC364: Marine fossils on mountains."

128. This is related to geotectonic movement, i.e., the lateral motion and pressure from continental plate collision. Various events that can be caused by such movement include local folding and faulting actions, area earthquakes, as well as more regional occurrences such as mountain uplift, expansion of rift depressions, and continental subduction action. When continental plates collide, sometimes mountains are formed by upward movement at the seams, while at other times rift valleys occur by downward movement at the seams. Sometimes there are even various degrees of combinations. As mentioned in a previous note, unlike with the moon (which is internally static), the Earth is geologically alive and constantly active.

129. The current official height of Mt. Everest is 29,029 ft. According to some studies, this shows an ongoing descending prominence from 29,041 (1999) to 29,035 (2010) to the above measurement. If these numbers are correct, then it shows a decrease of twelve feet in twenty years. (Be aware that these heights are based on the peak prominence itself and not the snow cap.) In fact, as of April 2019, another new survey effort was being planned to determine if the mountain had been yet further reduced during a recent earthquake. See Daley, "Nepalese Expedition Seeks to Find Out if an Earthquake Shrunk Mount Everest."

movement is ongoing and constant), most of the current familiar mountain formations (largely caused by tectonic collisions) were already prominently in place before 1.81 Ma.[130] Therefore, if the Flood occurred *after* the mountains uplifted (which we believe to be the case), it is logical to conclude that at least some of the mountaintop fossils may be of Noahic origin. Furthermore, as to Isaak's concern about recessional erosion cleansing away diluvial debris, in light of the orogenesis-*before*-Flood chronology, the mere fact that marine fossils currently exist on mountaintops (regardless of how they got there) is certainly evidence that not all Flood debris are prone to wash down from higher elevations as the waters recede.[131] Perhaps researchers, including both the advocates of Flood Geology and the advocates of current scientific orthodoxy, need to be more wary of taking an absolutist approach when speaking of certain workings of the natural order. When speaking of fossils, strata, and subaerial debris, "all" can become a very big word. The mere presence of marine debris in unique places (like mountaintops) makes diluvial causation a very real possibility.

The Deep Water in the Earth

What about all that water? This is probably the question most often asked by those skeptical of a global Flood. It is actually a very good question. After all, Ross posits the thought that it would take at least four and a half times the amount of water presently on the face of the Earth to accommodate a global Flood event.[132] Of course, Ross is referring to all the water on the surface of the planet, including glacial ice. William Robert Johnston, as part of his research on global warming and its possible effects,[133] asks the interesting question: "What if all the ice melts?"[134] He states:

> If all the icecaps in the world were to melt, sea level would rise about 60–75 meters (200–250 feet). This could not result from modern human activities, and from any realistic cause would take thousands of years to occur.... Currently the Earth has permanent ice in the icecaps of Antarctica and Greenland, plus much smaller permanent glaciers in various mountain regions of the world. This

130. McNamara, "Neogene," 388.

131. This issue also needs to be viewed in light of the Moshier study, which potentially suggests a lesser impact of detritus wash during water recession.

132. Ross, *The Genesis Question*, 152.

133. See Johnston, "Facts and figures on sea level rise," 1–3.

134. Johnston, "'What if all the ice melts?,'" 1–9.

ice is "permanent," however, only over the short timespan of modern human civilization. Additionally, there are two large ice sheets floating in seas off Antarctica, plus floating pack ice in the Arctic Ocean and surrounding Antarctica. Geological evidence indicates very clearly that at times in the Earth's past icecaps were much larger in extent—and alternately, at other times icecaps were virtually nonexistent.[135]

From a global perspective, all the surficial ice on Earth—both grounded and floating—is only about two percent of the planet's total surface water.[136] The current continental landmass is about 148 million square kilometers (with about 16 million square kilometers covered by glacial ice). If the sea were to rise about sixty-six meters, about 13 million square miles of land outside of Antarctica would become flooded. Of course, this also means that without the ice, Antarctica and Greenland would again become ice-free land (with about half of Antarctica underwater).[137] This translates into a world with a global landmass of, at least, 128 million square kilometers of dry land as compared to the current 132 million square kilometers (a mere difference of four million square kilometers).[138] This means that the Earth would by no means become globally flooded and the population of the world would not drown. In fact, as strange as it sounds, the living area of humanity might would actually increase. Johnston adds this further thought:

> As a result, in terms of total habitable land area, the Earth might have more than today. The coastal areas reclaimed by the sea would be mostly offset by now habitable areas of Greenland and Antarctica. Again, remember that such climate change would take thousands of years. Over such time scales vegetation would be restored to newly ice-free regions even without human activity. Also, vast areas which are now desert and tundra would become more fit for human habitation and agriculture.[139]

He continues:

---

135. Johnston, "'What if all the ice melts?,'" 1.
136. Johnston, "'What if all the ice melts?,'" 3.
137. Johnston, "'What if all the ice melts?,'" 7. With this thought, please also remember the reality of isostatic rebound. If the massive ice on these areas were to melt, the land would begin the process of isostatic uplift in proportion to the lessening of the glacial load.
138. Johnston, "'What if all the ice melts?,'" 7.
139. Johnston, "'What if all the ice melts?,'" 7.

> So why wouldn't people drown? . . . Over generations people would migrate as the coasts changed. Consider that virtually all of the settlements in the United States were established only in the last 350 years. Of course, many settlements inhabited for thousands of years would have to be abandoned to the ocean—just as many would have to be abandoned if ice age conditions returned and covered vast areas with ice sheets. But people can comfortably adjust where they live over periods of decades, far shorter than the thousands of years needed for these climate changes to naturally take place.[140]

While this knowledge should be quite comforting to the human race, especially in this time of increasing concern for the phenomenon of global warming, it does seem to confirm the idea that a global Noahic Flood may be "geophysically impossible."[141]

So, the question again is raised: If the Flood were global, what about all that water? Where did the water come from and where did it all go? There seems to be only two logical possibilities. Either God created it *ex nihilo* just for the Flood event and then gradually uncreated it afterwards, or the water used was always part of the original creation and possibly still exists somewhere in the natural order to this day.

There is no doubt that God could have specially created a large amount of additional water just for the Noahic Flood and then removed it again afterwards. The omnipotent God who created the universe with his Word (John 1:1–3)[142] could have certainly provided some new water for a special occasion. However, the scriptural text (Gen 7:11) does seem to imply that the water used came from natural sources: the "fountains of the great deep" and the "windows of heaven." In context, these descriptions are Hebrew euphemisms for subterranean (underground) and aerial (atmospheric) sources. There is a strong theological connection between this Noahic phenomenology and the separation of waters associated with the "firmament" in the creation text phenomenology of Genesis 1:7: "God made the firmament and separated the waters which were *under* the firmament from the waters which

---

140. Johnston, "'What if all the ice melts?,'" 7.

141. Ross, *The Genesis Question*, 160.

142. See John 1:3. Referring to the Word (Greek *logos*)—here not referencing mere speech, but the living God himself in action—this text states that "all things were *made* through him." The term translated as "made" is the Greek *ginomai*, which literally means "came into being." Our point is that in this passage (1:3), John is making a direct reference to the Hebrew *bara* (not Hebrew *asah*) concept in the creation narrative of Genesis 1. The implication of the text is a definitive *creation ex nihilo*. For more on this, see Copan and Craig, *Creation out of Nothing* (2004).

were *above* the firmament." Reflecting this, the image presented in the Genesis 7:11 text is the concept of *under* and *above* (everywhere) totality. This is a commonly used Hebraic devise (emphasizing totality) found in various forms elsewhere in Scripture, including in the New Testament (e.g., Acts 2:5—"devout men from every nation under heaven"; Phil 2:10—"every knee ... in heaven and on earth and under the earth"; Col 1:15—"all things ... in heaven and on earth, visible and invisible"; Col 1:20—"all things, whether on earth or in heaven"; etc.). When the divine judgment was initiated, water began coming from everywhere—from up, from down, from all around.[143] Except by God's special provision (i.e., the Ark), there was no way to avoid it and no way to ultimately escape it. The textual imagery seems to convey that God used massive rain storms and gushing aquifers to inundate the Earth. Therefore, it is our contention that the additional water used in the Noahic Flood was already in existence and is still in the natural order to this day. It is just not plainly visible and it is not all currently surficial.

If Ross is correct in his assertion that it would take about four and a half times the current volume of surface water to cover the planet (including the world's "highest mountains"),[144] there would have to be an enormous amount of water stored somewhere. Where could that water be? Back in 1997, Louis Bergeron presented the results of some astounding scientific research. He reported:

> [M]ore than 400 kilometers inside the Earth there may be enough water to replace the surface oceans more than ten times. But this water is not a series of immense seas. Rather, it is scattered in droplets, some as small as a single molecule, with most trapped inside crystal lattices of rare minerals that only form under intense pressures. How much there is down there is still fiercely debated. But these inner "oceans" could help to explain long-standing puzzles about Earth's formation, the causes of deep earthquakes hundreds of kilometers inside the Earth, and why massive volcanic outbursts suddenly flood hundreds of thousands of square kilometers with lava. They may even give a glimpse of what the future holds for the Earth's climate—and if we might ever be drowned from below.[145]

---

143. See Rashi, *Bereishis*, 75. He affirms that "God is here punishing measure for measure" because "the wickedness of man was great" [Gen 6:5]; "they [humanity] were stricken ... by the *great* deep" (italics his). In other words, the depth of great evil resulted in the commensurate depth of great judgment. In this case, Rashi avers that it was administered in a literal matching fashion. We concur with this assessment.

144. Ross, *The Genesis Question*, 152.

145. Bergeron, "Deep Waters," 22–26, esp. 22.

The Genesis Cataclysm

Yet, even before this, other scientists had suggested the existence of a hidden water supply—stored in hydrous minerals and hydrous melts—somewhere deep within the realm of the Earth's mantle.[146]

Since Bergeron's report, there have been several other significant discoveries as well. In 1999, a large "blob" of concentrated matter was found in the Earth's mantle located under the western Caribbean Sea about 500 miles below the sea floor. Using seismic wave reflections, the blob was described by geophysicists Ileana Madalina Tibuleac and Eugene Herrin as "anomalous matter" with "inhomogeneities" appearing to be "slowly descending vertically" deeper into the planet. It was identified as a subducted lithospheric slab with some unique characteristics.[147] This finding was significant because scientists had long since believed that the lower mantle of the Earth consisted of a homogeneous substance; the Tibuleac-Herrin study caused researchers to begin seriously questioning the common ideas about lower mantle composition.[148]

As a result, a whole new wave of mantle studies began to take place. For instance, scientific research (2002) carried on by Motohiko Murakami et al. suggested that a zone may exist between the crust and the mantle that acts as a vast water reservoir. Commensurate with the Bergeron report (as well as that of Jeanloz), Murakami posits that such a reservoir may hold from five to ten times the amount of water as that on the Earth's surface.[149]

Later, in 2006, Jesse F. Lawrence and Michael E. Wysession used seismic attenuation tomography to identify another anomaly (similar to that in the Tibuleac-Herrin report) some 620 miles under the Earth below China. It was determined that this anomaly is a subducted slab saturated with a

---

146 See Thompson, "Water in the Earth's Upper Mantle," 295–302. According to Thompson: "Experiments on the stability of hydrous minerals likely to be present in the Earth's mantle provide constraints on the distribution of water in the mantle, and the form in which it is stored. In regions of elevated mantle temperature, water may be stored not in minerals but in melts: such hydrous melts are important metasomatizing agents, and can induce volcanism beneath thick cratonic lithosphere" (295). Also, see Jeanloz, "The Hidden Shore," 26–31. According to Jeanloz, "Just as many astronomers think most of the mass in the universe is made up of invisible dark matter, a growing number of geologists, and I am among them, are becoming convinced that most of the water on earth may lie unseen, deep below the surface, dissolved into the rocks of the mantle and the core" (26).

147. Tibuleac and Herrin, "Lower Mantle Lateral Heterogeneity Beneath the Caribbean Sea," 1711–15. Also, see Shultz, "Large Blob Discovered Deep in the Earth," 30.

148. Shultz, "Large Blob Discovered Deep in the Earth," 30.

149. Murakami et al., "Water in Earth's Lower Mantle," 1885–87; cf. Bergeron, "Deep Waters," 22.

The Evidence of Nature

huge amount of water. Seismic attenuation testing showed that the volume of water in the "China Anomaly" is at least equivalent to the volume of the Arctic Ocean. Scientists have now come to believe that the subduction of cold lithospheric slabs with high-pressure hydrous phases (i.e., water containment) is a mechanism by which the Earth's mantle becomes hydrated.[150] Similarly to Murakami, Lawrence and Wysession surmised that the lower mantle—either through "primitive reservoirs," or through some sort of circulatory system—may contain up to five times the water as that found on the Earth's surface.[151]

Another significant advancement was the substantiation that ringwoodite (a mineral that is a high-pressure hydrous phase of olivine[152]) is not just of meteoritic origins (as was once thought), but also native to the planet Earth. The mineral was first found terrestrially in Brazil (2008) embedded within a rough diamond.[153] Ringwoodite, now known to be a mantle rock, traps and stores water. In fact, according to Pearson, vast amounts of ringwoodite located in the "deep Earth" is now thought to be the ultimate source of the planet's entire hydrosphere.[154] If this is true, it means that even the plainly visible surficial oceans actually had their initial origins in the subterranean "oceans."

Moreover, the widespread notion in science concerning the existence of a sub-crustal water zone was recently (2014) confirmed by the Schmandt study, which determined the existence of a "mantle transition zone—410 to 660 km below Earth's surface—[which] acts as a large reservoir of water."[155] According to Schmandt:

> The water cycle involves more than just the water that circulates between the atmosphere, oceans, and surface waters. It extends deep into the Earth's interior as the oceanic crust subducts, or slides,

---

150. Lawrence and Wysession, "Seismic Evidence for Subduction-Transported Water in the Lower Mantle," 251–61. Also, see Bolfan-Casanova, "Water in the Earth's mantle," 229–57.

151. Lawrence and Wysession, "Seismic Evidence for Subduction-Transported Water in the Lower Mantle," 251.

152. For further, see Bates and Jackson, "Olivine," 355. Olivine is the main mineral component of the Earth's upper mantle.

153. Pearson et al., "Hydrous mantle transition zone indicated by ringwoodite included within diamond," 221–24. Also, see Sample, "Rough Diamond hints at vast quantities of water inside Earth," 1–3.

154. Pearson et al., "Hydrous mantle transition zone indicated by ringwoodite included within diamond," 221.

155. Schmandt et al. "Dehydration melting at the top of the lower mantle," 1265.

under adjoining plates of crust and sinks into the mantle, carrying water with it.[156]

The water of the planet is active in both its exterior and interior dimensions. This is precisely what Steve Jacobsen, a geophysicist from Northwestern University (who was also part of the Schmandt study), calls the "whole-Earth water cycle."[157]

Here are a few astounding thoughts. Jacobsen asserts: "If just one percent of the weight of mantle rock located in the transition zone was water, it [alone] would be equivalent to nearly three times the amount of water in our [surface] oceans."[158] He also adds, "If [the stored water] wasn't there, it would be on the surface of the Earth, and mountaintops would be the only land poking out."[159] Note that Jacobsen's observation is assuming the very minimal (i.e., stored water = 1% weight of mantle rock = three times current surficial water) possibility. Scientists have determined that ringwoodite is capable of holding water up to 2.5–3% of its weight. This means that there could very well even exist a much greater quantity of mantle water (stored water = up to 3% weight of mantle rock = up to nine times current surficial water) inside the Earth.[160] If that amount of water were to be released on the Earth's surface, even the very mountaintops would become submerged. The truth is this: Though we do not really know with great precision just how much water is truly inside our planet, we do know that it is of an unquestionably *massive* volume.

The composite conclusion of these studies shows that the water volume stored inside the Earth may be as much as *five to ten* times that found in the surface oceans.[161] (It could possibly be even more than that.) Therefore, it plausibly appears that an excess (perhaps an astoundingly *significant* excess) of the necessary water volume required (which is four and a half times the amount of existing surficial water, as estimated by Ross[162]) for a global inundation is currently stored in the Earth below us. It is interesting that this

---

156. Schmandt et al. "Dehydration melting at the top of the lower mantle," 1265.

157. Davey, "Earth may have underground 'ocean' three times that on surface," 1.

158. Davey, "Earth may have underground 'ocean' three times that on surface," 1. Here Davey quotes Jacobsen in an interview.

159. Davey, "Earth may have underground 'ocean' three times that on surface," 2. Again, Davey quotes Jacobsen in an interview.

160. Ye et al., "Compressibility and thermal expansion of hydrous ringwoodite with 2.5(3) wt% H2O," 573–82.

161. Murakami et al., "Water in Earth's Lower Mantle," 1885–87.

162. Ross, *The Genesis Question*, 152.

incomprehensibly huge supply of water is variously described by researchers as "these inner oceans" (Bergeron) and "the hidden shore" (Jeanloz). It is also important not to forget the assertion of modern science that the Earth was once completely covered by a global ocean during the Archaean Eon (c. 3.8 Ga) until the beginning of the Paleoproterozoic Era (c. 2.5 Ga), and then having only very sparse, unstable, and uninhabitable land protrusions up through the time of the mid-Ordovician Period (c. 475 Ma) of the Phanerozoic Eon.[163] This lends some additional degree of credence to the notion of global Flood logistics.

Furthermore, on an intriguing peripheral note, modern science has posited that the majority of the Earth's hydrosphere was probably present in the planet's raw materials from the very beginning.[164] Recent computer modeling studies (2010) by chemist Nora H. de Leeuw et al. suggest that the raw materials were capable of holding onto water even in the midst of incredible proto-Earth temperatures.[165] This postulation is certainly corroborative with the strong pictorial "water world" imagery of Genesis 1:2. Perhaps there is very good reason to doubt Ross's view that a global inundation is geophysically impossible.

The Flood Fit at the Former Pliocene-Pleistocene Boundary

For the Noahic Flood to be considered as an historical event, it obviously must have actually occurred at some point in chronological time. Therefore, in this section we will show why it seems plausible to suggest that the Flood occurred at just prior to 1.81 Ma in our Old-Earth paradigm. We will examine this notion both evidentially and inferentially.

The boundary between the Pliocene and Pleistocene epochs until somewhat recently was set at the Gelasian-Calabrian stage boundary (1.81 Ma). This is the point in the natural record that shows evidence of very definitive and "well marked" glacial-interglacial cycles.[166] However, it should be noted

    163. See Shiga, "Ancient Earth was a barren waterworld," 8; also, see Bergeron, "Stanford Study: Earth's early ocean cooled more than a billion years earlier than thought."
    164. Shiga, "Earth may have had water from day one," 12. This postulation, of course, seems to be confirmed by the aforementioned Pearson ringwoodite study (2014).
    165. de Leeuw et al., "Where on Earth has our water come from?." De Leeuw et al. states: "The presence of water in the Earth has long been an enigma. However, computer modeling techniques have shown that the absorption of water onto fractal surfaces of interplanetary dust particles, which are present in the planetary accretion disk, is sufficiently strong to provide a visible origin of terrestrial water."
    166. McGowran et al., "Neogene and Quaternary coexisting in the geological time

that in June 2009, the epochal boundary was formally moved backward to include the full Gelasian Stage as part of the Pleistocene Epoch (removing it from the preceding Pliocene Epoch). This means that the beginning of the Pleistocene Epoch—the traditional Ice Age epoch—is currently now set earlier at 2.58 Ma.[167] The reasons for the formal boundary move involve multiple empirical events that are associated with that geochronological point: i.e., a key magnetic polarity reversal of the Earth (the Gauss-Matuyama geomagnetic reversal), several significant paleontologic events involving microfossils (the last appearance of some and the first appearance of others), as well as the very earliest signs of a new severe climactic cooling trend (e.g., the Northern hemisphere ice sheets began an expansion)—even though the definitive glacial cycles did not fully manifest widespread until some 770,000

---

scale: The inclusive compromise," 9. McGowran affirms that there were both glacials and warming trends prior to the Pliocene-Pleistocene boundary, but even so the Gelasian-Calabrian Stage is climatically "well marked." They also aver that there are strong climactic markers at more recent points in time, notably in the mid-Pleistocene (0.6 Ma) that indicate increased Ice Age conditions (9). This seems to confirm that the cyclic glacial event beginning at 1.81 Ma continued to intensify through 0.6 Ma and beyond. For further corroborative detail, also see Cita et al., "The Calabrian Stage redefined," 408–19 (December 2008). They state: "Increasing evidence obtained both from the terrestrial record (southern extension of the glacial fronts in the Northern Hemisphere, the onset of loess deposition in China) and from the oceans (the presence of ice-rafted debris in the North Atlantic and North Pacific, isotopic evidence of progressive cooling) indicated that a combination of paleogeographic (closure of the Panama isthmus), paleooceanographic (enhancement of meridian currents), and extra-terrestrial forcing resulted in a rapid collapse [at 1.806 Ma] of the already deteriorating Pliocene climactic conditions, corroborating the concept of the "ice age" as indicated in the Northern Hemisphere" (410).

167. Gibbard et al., "Formal Ratification of the Quaternary System/Period and the Pleistocene Series/Epoch with a base at 2.58 Ma," 96–102.

years later.[168] While the decision by the IUGS/ICS[169] is certainly understandable, for our purposes, however, the boundary move is merely somewhat of a paper tiger. It does not significantly affect the assertions of this project since the 1.81 million-year point (following Cita) is indeed associated with a notable climactic event, viz., the advent of definitive and strong cyclic glaciation (MIS 44, 42, 40), which gradually intensified through a glacial maximum at 0.6 Ma (MIS 18, 16, 14) and then carried on in a fluctuating, but overall reducing fashion until the present Holocene Epoch at 11.7 ka;[170] and, thus our postulation does not depend upon the *formal* placement of this time period.[171]

168. See Aguirre and Pasini, "The Pliocene-Pleistocene Boundary," 116–120. As to this formal boundary change, they explain: "The definition of the beginning of the Pleistocene no longer has a primary climactic implication, which, because of latitudinal and altitudinal effects on world climate, would be difficult to provide. In some area[s] the earliest glacial periods will be Pliocene age, or even older; in others they will be of mid-Pleistocene age" (119). In other words, the glaciation events tended to be regionally uneven and thus scientists were seeking a more accurately *fixed* reference point for the epochal boundary that was not fundamentally and solely based on climate. The new Pleistocene boundary—at 2.58 Ma (which begins the Gelasian Stage)—is set at the point of several notable events: the Gauss-Matuyama magnetic reversal, an MIS glacial stage, and the extinctions of certain marine organisms (coccoliths—calcareous marine algae), including *Discoaster pentaradiatus* and *Discoaster surculus*. This is the approximate point when the ice sheets in the Northern Hemisphere first began to expand. Note that the Aguirre-Pasini article is from 1985 and the formal change did not occur until 2009. The discussion to resolve these boundary issues has actually had been going on for decades (e.g., see Gibbard et al., "What status for the Quaternary?," 1–6). Also, as per Cita's comment in the note above, this change does not negate the significance of the 1.81 Ma (1.806 Ma) boundary point—which does have climactic significance and which is very material to our paradigm.

169. International Union of Geological Sciences / International Commission on Stratigraphy; the ICS is a sub-commission of the IUGS. The IUGS has a professional membership of over a million geoscientists and sponsors the International Geological Congress, which gathers every four years. For more info, see: https://www.iugs.org.

170. See McGowran et al., "Neogene and Quaternary Co-existing," 9. Note that the 1.806 Ma timeline also has its own notable non-climactic boundary markers as well: this is the point in time of the extinction of certain marine creatures, including *Discoaster brouweri* (coccolith), *Globigerinoides obliquus extremus* (foraminifer), and *Calcidiscus macintyrei* (nannoplankton); it is also the point in time of the first appearance of *Gephyrocapsa oceanica* (nannoplankton) (see Aquirre and Pasini, "The Pliocene-Pleistocene Boundary," 119). There is also association at this boundary with the Olduvai magnetic reversal event.

171. Chronostratigraphic boundaries, particularly Quaternary boundaries, remain in ongoing debate. For instance, see Gibbard and Head, "The Definition of the Quaternary System/Era and the Pleistocene Series/Epoch," 125–33; and "The newly-ratified definition of the Quaternary System/Period and redefinition of the Pleistocene Series/

In our paradigm, humanity first appeared at approximately 1.9 Ma (i.e., the earliest currently known evidence of *Homo erectus*).[172] With our postulation that the Noahic Flood occurred at some point just prior to the 1.81 Ma boundary, we apply a modified OEC application of the Oard Model. According to Oard's postulation, the conditions on the Earth would be very conducive to Ice Age-type glaciation within 200 to 1,700 years after a global flood event (with about 500 years most probable).[173]

There are at least three features in the natural record at the 1.81 Ma point that should be considered. First, there are certain signs of significant ephemeral sedimentary deposition at various intercontinental locations. Second, there is also the timing of first humanity combined with the beginning of the definitive glacial-interglacial cycles that have been strongly used to identify the traditional Ice Age. Third, there are some peripheral lithographic markers that seem to be confirming of the time fit.

Though there is no definitive Noahic stratification in the geologic record (see previous section in this chapter),[174] there are isolated pockets of mappable water-related (including glacial) ephemeral and unconsolidated (e.g., some regolithic material, etc.) sedimentary deposition (the alluvium is often intermixed with other forms) throughout the world classified as late Pliocene and

---

Epoch, and comparison of proposals advanced prior to formal ratification," 152–58. Of course, the Tertiary Period is definitely not immune either; see also, Head et al., "The Tertiary: a proposal for its formal definition," 248–50. (Poor Giovani Arduino!)

172. For further explanation concerning our basis of this timeline for first humanity, please see, "The Defining of Humankind," in *The Genesis Column* (111–16).

173. Oard, "A Post-Flood Ice-Age Model can Account for Quaternary Features," 8–26. As to the requirements for Ice Age glaciation, see Clark, *Fossils, Flood, and Fire*, 178, 180. Clark avers: "Contrary to common opinion, a glacial period would not require long cold winters, but rather cool damp summers. It has been calculated that a difference of 5 degrees Fahrenheit from the present annual average, other factors being favorable, would be sufficient to bring on glaciation. Perhaps even more important than the temperature factor is that of moisture. In order for glaciation to occur, abundant precipitation would be necessary. This situation was apparently amply met in the years following the Flood" (178). The combined elements of cool, damp summers and abundant precipitation coupled with the probability that the Flood/post-Flood oceans were extremely warm (having predominantly originated from the inner recesses of the Earth) would have been extremely conducive to the development of expansive glaciation as the waters slowly cooled and receded over time.

174. This is, as opposed, for instance, to the worldwide distribution of an explicit iridium deposition located at the Cretaceous-Tertiary boundary, which is indicative of catastrophic asteroidal impact at 65.5 Ma (see Schulte et al., "The Chicxulub Asteroid Impact and Mass Extinction at the Cretaceous-Paleogene Boundary," 1214–18). NOTE: Just to avert confusion, the Cretaceous-Tertiary (K-T) boundary is the traditional name for what is also known today as the Cretaceous-Paleogene (K-Pg) boundary.

early Pleistocene. Some such locations include the Middle Atlantic Coastal Plain of Delaware, Maryland, and Virginia (designated: lagoon and fluvial deposits),[175] northern and western Kentucky (designated: thin surficial veneer in three sequences—high-level fluvial deposits with underlying Pliocene and Pleistocene terraces; Pleistocene glacial deposits and loess; and alluvium that underlies Pleistocene and Holocene terraces and flood plains),[176] Arizona (designated: thin Quaternary stream deposits over much older deposits),[177] Central Kansas (designated: algal limestone alluvial deposits),[178] Western Australia (designated: unlithified carbonate deposits on a marine erosional surface),[179] Wanganui Basin, New Zealand (designated: Pliocene-Pleistocene cyclothemic marine sedimentary fill),[180] the Lihue Basin in Kauai, Hawaii (designated: fossiliferous marine deposits),[181] the Laguna Salada basin in northwestern Mexico (designated: three sequences—marine mudstone; non-marine redbeds consisting of breccia, conglomerate, conglomerate sandstone and fine-grained sandstone and mudstone; and uncemented boulder gravel),[182] the Southern Apennines of Italy (designated: sub-aqueous volcanic deposits made up of ashy pyroclasts),[183] the Siena Basin of the Northern Apennines in Italy (designated: upper Pliocene fluvial valley fill, encased within shallow marine deposits from the middle Pliocene and bedrock from pre-Neogene),[184]

---

175. Ramsey, "Distribution of Late Pliocene and Quaternary Deposits in the Middle Atlantic Coastal Plain."

176. McDowell and Newell, "Quaternary System." From a diluvial perspective, these sequences could represent Flood deposits and post-Flood glacial deposition.

177. Richard et al., "Early Pleistocene to late Miocene basin deposits."

178. Frye, "Valley erosion since Pliocene 'algal limestone' deposition in Central Kansas," 1–12.

179. James and Bone, "A Late Pliocene-Early Pleistocene, inner-shelf, subtropical, seagrass-dominated carbonate," 343–59.

180. Naish and Kamp, "Pliocene-Pleistocene marine cyclothems, Wanganui Basin, New Zealand," 223–43.

181. Izuka and Resig, "Evidence of Late Pliocene-Early Pleistocene marine environments in the deep subsurface of the Lihue Basin, Kauai, Hawaii," 442–51.

182. Dorsey and Martin-Barajas, "Sedimentation and deformation in a Pliocene-Pleistocene transtentional supradetachment basin, Laguna Salada, north-west Mexico," 205–21. From a diluvial perspective, these three sequences can possibly be interpreted as [1] Flood deposition, [2] post-Flood erosion, and [3] post-Flood glacial debris.

183. Prosser et al., "Late Pliocene volcaniclastic products from Southern Apennines," 521–36. This is included because some have associated volcanism with the Noahic Flood, particularly in its initiatory stages.

184. Aldinucci et al., "Climactic and tectonic signature in the fluvial infill of a Late Pliocene valley," 398–414.

The Genesis Cataclysm

Northern Italy (designated: marine deposits),[185] Peri-Adriatic Basin, Central Italy (designated: submarine canyon fills),[186] and Trinidad (designated: deltaic sediments).[187] There are many others as well; these particulars are just a cross-section of reports indicating examples of late Pliocene-early Pleistocene, i.e., Gelasian-Calabrian boundary, (water-related) ephemeral deposition. The point is that it is very possible that some ephemeral alluvial deposition from the Noahic Flood might still exist in the intercontinental natural record. Whether any of this deposition can ever be clearly identified in the mix as Noahic is uncertain and at this point in time improbable; yet alluvial sedimentation does substantially exist in various significant and mappable samples in the vicinity of the old Pliocene-Pleistocene transition point.[188]

Keep in mind also the results of Clarey's study showing the significant carbonate presence which peaks at this same proximate stratigraphic location.[189] Interestingly, there have also been coccoliths[190] found in frozen Arctic sediments which have been dated as late Pliocene-early Pleistocene.[191] These calcium carbonate deposits at this particular geochronological location could possibly be linked to Noahic/glacial transition.

Another fascinating caveat involves the primary lithographic foundation of the Vrica formation: marine claystone.[192] According to Aguirre and Pasini:

---

185. Pervesler et al., "Ichnological record of environmental changes in Early Quaternary (Gelasian-Calabrian) marine deposits of the Stirone Section, Northern Italy," 578–93.

186. Di Celma et al., "Sedimentology, architecture, and sequence stratigraphy of coarse-grained, submarine canyon fills from Pleistocene (Gelasian-Calabrian) of the Peri-Adriatic Basin, central Italy," 1340–65.

187. Tyson, "A Model for the Late Pliocene Tectonics and its Effects on Quaternary Sedimentation in the Trinidad Area of the East Venezuelan Basin."

188. Also, see Cita et al., 411. They assert that "Sediment accumulation rates are high" at the base of the Calabrian Stage.

189. Clarey, "Local Catastrophes or Receding Floodwater? Global Geologic Data that refute a K-Pg (K-T) Flood/post-Flood Boundary," 100–20.

190. Coccoliths are plates of calcium carbonate formed by eucharotic phyto-plankton (coccolithophores), which are single-cell marine algae.

191. Worsley and Herman, "Episodic Ice-Free Arctic Ocean in Pliocene and Pleistocene Time: Calcareous Nannofossil Evidence," 323–25.

192. Claystone is one of several varieties of mudrock. Others include slate, shale, siltstone, etc. They fall into the sedimentary category and are the most pervasive form of rock deposit on Earth. It is often affiliated with alluvium or calcareous ooze. See Bates and Jackson, *Dictionary of Geological Terms*, 92.

The Evidence of Nature

> The Vrica section . . . consists of open sea deposits preserved in the emergent portion of a late Cenozoic sedimentary basin. The rocks are bathyal, marly and silty claystones (dark grey or blue-grey in colour) with interbedded, fairly conspicuous, pale grey-pink sapropelic marker beds.[193]

This indicates that the primary stratotype (i.e., the designated rock formation used to identify the lower stage boundary of a particular chronostratigraphic sequence)[194] for the Gelasian-Calabrian boundary is well suffused with *marine* markers. It should also be noted that the Vrica stratotype can be extensively and precisely correlated with other such marine geological sequences throughout the world.[195] This is declarative of the global significance of the 1.806 Ma boundary.

Furthermore, it is also certainly possible that some ephemeral sedimentation designated as early Holocene (which is just *above* our proposed geochronological point) could be Noahic as well since the Flood event (followed by the Ice Age with its sediment/debris modification and redistributive action) happened so recently in relative time.[196] Due to the fleetingness

---

193. Aguirre and Pasini, "The Pliocene-Pleistocene Boundary," 116–20.

194. See Bates and Jackson, "stratotype," 495. Also known as a GSSP = Global Boundary Stratotype Section and Point. For further on this subject, see Smith et al., "GSSPs, global stratigraphy and correlation," 37–68.

195. Aguirre and Passini, "The Pliocene-Pleistocene Boundary," 119. See also, Maiorano et al., "Vrica-Crotone and Montalbano Jonico sections: A potential unit-stratotype of the Calabrian Stage," 218–33. Maiorano identifies another corresponding lithographic section in Basilicata, Italy.

196. See Clark, *Fossils, Flood, and Fire*, 182–86. Here he states: "The older drift [i.e., usually associated with the first three of the traditional four glacials: Nebraskan, Kansan, and Illinoan] lacks topographic expression, but is spread out thinly and widely, and has been so eroded and covered with wind-blown loess that its identification is exceedingly difficult. It lacks morainic characteristics. Pebbles contained in it are often well rounded, suggesting water action. As a rule it is weathered more than the newer drift, and this has been taken as evidence for a longer time of exposure to the elements. However, when we realize that after the Flood the climate was semi-tropic quite far north, we can understand how some materials left over from that catastrophe might show a high degree of weathering. It may be possible that some of this material represents debris of that nature, although probably not entirely. . . . In contrast with the older drift, the newer, or Wisconsin, shows strong glacial topography—eskers, kames moraines, outwash plains, striations, etc. Water-sorted material is abundant, and little denudation has taken place since its deposition." The point is that it is improbable to absolutely and precisely identify much of the sedimentation and debris (particularly the older drift) at this point in the natural record. Clark implies that some of the older deposits could be Noahic related, while the newer deposits are more definitively the result of post-Flood glaciation. A post-Flood glaciation would have certainly affected extant Noahic sedimentation.

of much sedimentary deposition, particularly that of the subaerial variety (and especially considering the possible effects of post-Flood glaciation upon the deposits), this is more of a supportive rather than a primary feature. Yet—it is, nonetheless, a feature.

The most important feature, by far, is the relational timing of humanity's advent (1.9 Ma) with the beginning of definitively strong glacial-interglacial cycles (1.81 Ma).[197] Such a timeline seems to be a good fit for the creation, fall, and degradation of humanity[198] leading up to the Flood event and subsequent

---

197. NOTE: Traditionally, the Quaternary Ice Age has been understood to include four glacial-interglacial cycles. This has been determined from continental (land) strata and other geological features; however, scientists have more recently determined that subaqueous (marine) strata and chemical evidence (esp., O18 and O16 in calcite shells, as well as strontium—a first cousin to calcium, and carbon isotopes, etc.) (see Veizer et al., "[E]volution of Phanerozoic seawater") provide more accurate data and reveal additional cycles (at least a fifth, maybe more). Therefore, Ice Age cycles are now more often identified by Marine Isotopic Stage (MIS) numbers (e.g., MIS 3, 7, 12, 16, etc.; sometimes they are also referred to as Oxygen Isotopic Stages: OIS numbers) than by regional geological names (e.g., Pre-Illinoian, Illinoian, Sangamonian, Wisconsin; Günz, Mindel, Riss, Würm, etc.). The stage numbers are representative of alternating cool periods and warm periods in the climactic history of the Quaternary Period (and, right now, up to nearly three and a half million years of the upper Tertiary Period). Scientists can, to some degree, extrapolate the paleoclimate by studying the oxygen isotopes in marine core samples and, from them, positing temperature data. The even MIS numbers represent the cold/glacial periods (core samples have high levels of oxygen-18) and the odd numbers represent the warmer/interglacial periods (core samples have low levels of oxygen-18).

198. For further on this human timeline fit, see Stallings, *The Genesis Column*, 116–17. Note this in particular: "Therefore, in this time placement paradigm, Adam would have existed at least 90,000 years (possibly much earlier) before the Noahic catastrophe... This time frame gives the historic Adam and Eve a significant opportunity to live and subsist in the pristine Edenic world (Gen 2:8–25) prior to the fall and subsequent advent of death and corruption (Gen 3); it also provides ample time (post-fall) for human sin to manifest itself into the extremely wicked pre-Flood conditions as recorded in Genesis 6:1–5" (117). There are some people who struggle with the idea of setting the historic Adam this far back in time. Often the primary locus of their difficulty involves the biblical genealogies. But, have no fear. A couple of clarifying points need to be made. [1] First, we do not believe that Adamic age was registered in chronological time until after the Fall. (Pre-Fall time existed only in perfect *kairos*—which innately involves eternity without temporality—and is thus generally incomprehensible to our temporal post-Fall experience and understanding.) Chronological limitation was one of the Fall's effectual and progressing consequences. Therefore, since there was no death in the pre-Fall creation, the very notion of age was essentially inapplicable. [2] Second, as to the significance of the genealogies of Genesis 5 and 11, see *The Genesis Column*, 107–10. The genealogical material of the ANE (that is, the Ancient Near East—of which the biblical genealogies are part and parcel with the corpora) is a very unique form of literature with a special style all its own. Keep in mind that these genealogies, including also the Noahic descendancy in the Table of Nations (Gen 10—which is actually a list with various groupings and not a true genealogy), should be considered

The Evidence of Nature

to be accurate in their general presentation, but just not complete in the same way as our contemporary (particularly, Western) sensibility would like to require. For instance, in addition to the prominent Cainan example (for this, compare Gen 11:12 with Luke 3:36–37 and Jub 8:1–2—and there are numerous other similar examples in the Bible), note also the repeated blanket statements as to the Adamic via Seth's (x9 = Gen 5:4, 7, 10, 13, 16, 19, 22, 26, 30) and the Noahic via Shem's (x8 = Gen 11:11, 13, 15, 17, 19, 21, 23, 25) unidentified and multiplicitous progeny—"and [he] had other [unspecified] sons and daughters"—on their genealogical journey to an Abrahamic destination (viz., Adam>Noah>Abraham). These stylistic methods—i.e., inclusive of omissions and indefinite statements, as well as intentionally enumerated and patterned generational alignments (frequently in 10- or 14-generation increments)—are actually common genealogical devices used in the works of the ANE which always indicate the reality of unknown gaps concerning people and time in the written recordings. (For a good read on this subject, see Steinmann, "Gaps in the Genealogies," 141–58.) Also, despite any very intentional generational gaps by an author, the ages listed and the number of years referenced (Hebrew *shanah* = year) are specified in the text to emphasize the actual *historical existence* of the primordial people listed, while the connective "begats" reveal the actual *directional destiny* of the primordial lineage (as opposed to providing merely a sterile report of a family tree, which from a veneer perspective, it appears cursorily to show; for instance, in Genesis 11:10–11, Shem is presented as the father of Arpachshad; he is indeed the father of Arpachshad, although Arpachshad *may* biologically be his son multiple generations into the future—which could be the case for many, if not all, of the listed names; in the ANE, "father" frequently means "ancestor," and "son" frequently means "descendent"). As such, each listed name serves as something akin to a periodic signpost along the genealogical highway with potential distances (generations)—even very long distances (perhaps many generations; e.g., see Ps 105:8)—between the posted signs (names). In typical form, these intentionally ordered genealogical narratives start with a *germinal name* (a beginning patriarch), conclude with a *terminal name* (an ending patriarch), and are interspersed in between with *seminal names* (only those people chosen as being most influential or otherwise significant within that patriarchal lineage). The designated germinal-to-terminal sequence progresses in a deliberately purposeful direction. The sequence is designed to direct the reader of the text to follow the signs (names) along the road until the intended destination is finally reached. While this practice of prosaic license may seem quite counterintuitive (or even troublesome) to our thinking today concerning what we perceive as accuracy, this antiquated practice is in no way meant to detract from the historicity of the text, but simply reflects the typical arrangement methodology of the ANE milieu concerning the recording of genealogical narratives (see Plichta, "Ancient Near Eastern Genealogies," for an excellent and concise essay addressing this very thing). Simply put, this is just how the ANE world did it. We must remember that God chose to reveal his eternal truth through the cultural and social mechanisms of that *other* people, time, and place (and not that of our own). Again, as mentioned in *The Genesis Column*, the purpose of these familial annals is not to be an absolute chronogenealogy (i.e., it will not serve in the same way as a modern ancestry archival tool, nor will it give us the dates for such things as the creation of the world, first humanity, the Flood, the Babelian dispersion, etc.), but rather to be a relational and connective signifier that points definitively in the direction of a specific and purposeful divine meta-narrative (i.e., where God is ultimately going with his grand program). As these genealogical texts are part of the particular revelation of God, they do, in fact, accomplish this intended purpose

Ice Age period.[199] Obviously, in any biblical model, humanity must precede the Flood, and in our model, the Flood must also precede the Ice Age. This does not mean that there was not already a cooling climate and even some long-term glaciation in existence prior to the Flood.[200] After all, mainstream science holds that Antarctica was glaciated to some degree possibly as early as the mid-Eocene Epoch (c. 45.5 Ma).[201] Furthermore, there are strong signs in the geologic record which indicate later periods of cooling during the Miocene Epoch and the Pliocene Epoch with a definitive climactic cooling trend initiated at about 2.58 Ma (which is the lower Gelasian Stage boundary).[202] This cooling trend, confirmed by oxygen isotopic evidence, led to the formation and expansion of some new glaciation (MIS 102–104) in the Northern Hemisphere.[203] Of course, in our purview, this glaciation is pre-Flood. Note

---

with the greatest of precision. We would do well to accept this purpose and thus not use the biblical genealogies to assert false truth or to overtly speculate on the chronogenealogically unknowable (1 Tim 1:4).

199. See Cvancara, *A Field Manual for the Amateur Geologist*, 20–22. He provides a good concise description of what is meant by the term, *the Ice Age*: "Today, glaciers cover about 10 percent of Earth's land surface; 90 percent of that ice is on Antarctica. But during the Pleistocene Epoch, which began about two million years ago, glaciers were more extensive. Their margins, however, fluctuated several times [glacial-interglacial cycles], to expand and encroach at one time [glacials], to melt back at another [interglacials]. The last extensive encroachment took place 20,000 to 15,000 years ago when glaciers covered 30 percent of Earth's land surface. Ice covered most of northern North America—including Canada, the northern United States, and Greenland—northern Europe and northern Asia, Antarctica, and southernmost South America. Glaciers on Antarctica and Greenland today remain as the most conspicuous remnants of the great Pleistocene ice sheet."

200. Many early geologists believed this to be the case. However, today, this notion seems to find itself in frequent contrast with YEC, which tends to lean toward a warmer pre-Flood climate; for instance, see Rush and Vardiman, "Pre-Flood Canopy Radiative Temperature Profiles," 2–3. Furthermore, YEC often denies the occurrence of any pre-Flood ice ages; for instance, see Snelling, *Earth's Catastrophic Past* (Vol. 2), 1023–29.

201. Ehrmann and Mackensen, "Sedimentological evidence for the formation of an East Antarctic ice sheet in Eocene/Oligocene Time," 85–112. Please note that there is not as much certainty as to the age of the current Arctic ice sheet, although it is thought to have been in existence since at least 700,000 ka (see *Worsley and Herman*, above) and possibly as early as 4 Ma (see Clark, "The Arctic Ocean and Post-Jurassic Paleoclimatology," 133).

202. See Gibbard and van Kolfschoten, "The Pleistocene and Holocene Epochs," 442. They state: "It can be argued that the first severe cold climate takes place at a stratigraphic position equivalent to the base of the Dutch terrestrial Praetiglian Stage, and some earth scientists studying Quaternary strata in northern Europe tend to begin their Pleistocene [Ice Age] at this level. . . . This older level corresponds to the Gauss/Matuyama magnetic epoch boundary (2.6 Ma) and the base of the Pliocene Gelasian Stage."

203. Climactic flux—even of a severe and very widespread nature—is nothing new.

that it is also possible that glaciation may have accompanied the Flood, especially in its early stages (but probably not for long due to the massive "bursting forth" increase of warm water from the Earth's subterranean aquifers and hydrothermal vents).

The matter of pre-Flood glaciation presents no problem for our Old-Earth Flood model. It is very important to note that, in our paradigm, the ancient ice caps or any new Miocene-Pliocene cooling trends are not directly causative of the cyclic glaciation event beginning post-Flood at 1.81 Ma. Cool air temperatures may be generally *related* in the sense of persisting to some extent (i.e., a carry-over) through the Flood-year, but not primarily *causative* to post-Flood conditions. In fact, if the meteorological logistics of the Oard model are correct, the earlier cooling trends—while perhaps on-going during the Flood-year—were obviously not *from* the same event (i.e., they were pre-existing and were of a quite different and long-term causation). After all, in our modified OEC application of the Oard model, the Flood—which we place just prior to 1.81 Ma—was the catalyst for the Quaternary Ice Age. The conclusion of the Flood would have progressively issued in a marked climactic collapse. The immediate conditions would have included a barren existence characterized by cold landmasses, yet reasonably warm oceans. The isotherms likely would have been radically even and consistent, particularly at the land/ocean interactions.[204] This would have been the springboard environment for rapid[205] climactic degradation.[206] In

---

Science has posited the possibility of "Snowball Earth" in the Neoproterozoic Era prior to 635 Ma (see Ogg et al., *The Concise Geologic Timescale*, 31–32; cf. Kirschvink, "Late Proterozoic Low-Latitude Global Glaciation: the Snowball Earth," 51–52), as well as later significant glaciation during the late Paleozoic Era (see Montanez and Poulsen, "The Late Paleozoic Ice Age: An Evolving Paradigm," 629–56; cf. Davis A. Young, *Creation and the Flood*, 205–6). Interestingly, this later event is known variously as the Karoo Ice Age and the late Paleozoic Icehouse.

204. Oard, *An Ice Age Caused by the Genesis Flood*, 46.

205. That is, *rapid* within a scientific context. As mentioned previously, Oard posits that it would likely take from 200 to 1,700 years post-Flood—with about 500 years most probable—for this degradation to become fully manifest (see Oard, "A Post-Flood Ice-Age Model," 7). Meanwhile, Clark favors about a 1,000-year post-Flood timing for maximum glaciation to occur (see Clark, *Fossils, Flood, and Fire*, 180). Note that both of these advocations fall within the same time window. Within the apertures of deep time, any sequence of two millennia or less is considered to be *extremely* rapid.

206. Interestingly, this post-Noahic process and associative effects seems to be very similar to what happened previously in Earth history with the appearance of the first stable land (Gondwana, c. 550/510 Ma) followed by the appearance of the first land plant life (Gondwana inhabitable, c. 475 Ma) during the late Ordovician Period (see *The Genesis Column*, "God Day Three," 76–83)—that is, at the final permanent recession of

any biblical paradigm, the sudden cataclysmic occurrence of a warm-water global Flood event would have progressively brought an end to any prior ancient glaciation—only then to be followed by new glacial formation and amplification in the successive post-Flood world. Again, for our purposes, the formal Pleistocene boundary move to 2.58 Ma is just a paper tiger (and is actually irrelevant to our paradigm). Indeed, when factoring in the Noahic Flood event, we believe that the Gelasian-Calabrian boundary (1.81 Ma) is a much more accurate point for the placement of the Flood-Ice Age transition.

It should also be noted that if anthropologists were to find *Homo erectus* remains earlier than those that have already been recovered (1.9 Ma)—which is possible, maybe even probable—then the advent of humanity could easily be moved incrementally backward in time to accommodate the new anthropological findings. This would cause no damage to our paradigm. It would not in any way affect the relationship between the Flood and the Ice Age, but would simply push the appearance of Adam further back in chronological time and widen the gap between Adam and Noah.

There are three other peripheral phenomena that seem to support this timeline fit. First, Rupke provides examples of polystrate trees in the Ruhr Valley of Germany that are actually preserved as stumps about 7.5 meters in height that "must have been still higher before they were cut down by

---

the primordial "water world." (Note that either the initial abundant appearance—or a recovering profusion—of new plant life can be an important contributive factor to the advent of glaciation due to the botanical inbreathing of carbon dioxide with the correlative outbreathing surfeit of oxygen; see, Lenton et al., "First plants cooled the Ordovician," 86–89; also, see Royer et al., "CO2 as a primary driver of Phanerozoic climate," 4.) A series of minor repetitive glacial events began occurring between 478 Ma and the time immediately prior to the Andean-Saharan Ice Age (c. 458–420 Ma) (see Frakes et al., *Climate Modes of the Phanerozoic*, 15–26, esp. 15–18; also, see Crowell, "Continental Glaciation through Geologic Times," 80). These glacial trends were likely parts of the progressive environmental collapse leading up to the maximum A-S glaciation. The Andean-Saharan event—inclusive of its progressively decreasing ocean temperature—notably coincided with the Ordovician-Silurian Extinction Event (c. 455–430 Ma), which brought the end to many taxa, including many brachiopods and trilobites, etc. The rise of the permanent land concurred with the significant decrease in sea level. Major sea level change is a crucial causative factor in the initiation of extensive glaciation, which then, in turn, results in the significant decrease of ocean temperatures. There would likely have been a dynamically similar (just with a much faster progression) scenario with the recession of the Noahic Flood. This faster progression is evidenced in Genesis 8:11 by the return of the dove with an olive leaf, showing an already beginning recovery of some land plant life. This is again similar to God Day Three (and no doubt divinely-induced). While the long-term early Earth "water world" and the short-term Noahic Flood are two different types of flood events, contextually speaking, there seems to be a number of comparative parallels that reasonably confirm the viability of the Noahic Flood-Quaternary Ice Age relationship.

[near] the Ruhr in the Riss glacial epoch."²⁰⁷ His point is that the trees were buried in multiple strata through some sort of catastrophic action and then later shaved down by the incisive advancement and recession of glaciation. This can be understood to be evidentially indicative that the Noahic Flood was indeed *followed* by the Ice Age (per Oard's model). Rupke presents other examples of this in other locations, including the Joggins Formation of Nova Scotia.²⁰⁸ He states that other such specific phenomena occur in the Earth's northern latitudes over a very widespread area.²⁰⁹

Second, there are two (now extinct) epeiric seas that fit this timeline as well. Both the Tyrrell Sea²¹⁰ and the Champlain Sea could very well have been residuals left behind from the Flood/Ice Age events. It is interesting that both seas existed from the late Pleistocene Epoch into the early Holocene Epoch, and both were largely located in the region of eastern Canada²¹¹—in the immediate path of the Laurentide Ice Sheet. The composite of these circumstantial evidences seems to support the placement of the Flood/Ice Age events at the old Pliocene-Pleistocene boundary (1.81 Ma).

Furthermore, a third potentially corroborative phenomenon involves an extensive Antarctic fossil forest (running "about 1,300 kilometers along the Transantarctic Mountains" and described as "a shrublike beach forest"²¹²) that has been estimated to be—*at most*—only about three million years old.²¹³ This particular forest is unique in that it exists in the midst of numerous other fossil forests that have been determined to be much older. The oldest Antarctic forests have been dated to at least 260 million years,

---

207. Rupke, "Prolegomena to a Study of Cataclysmal Sedimentation," 153. The Riss Glacial is the third glacial cycle in the European Alpine regional sequence. Note our earlier reference to this older form of regional geological glacial identification in relation to the now more frequent use of Marine Isotope Stages (MIS).

208. Rupke, "Prolegomena to a Study of Cataclysmal Sedimentation," 153–54. Keep in mind, however, our earlier note disparaging the use of polystrate trees as a general evidence of the Noahic Flood. We refer here only to very specific examples for very specific reasons.

209. Rupke, "Prolegomena to a Study of Cataclysmal Sedimentation," 153.

210. Be reminded that the present Hudson Bay is a relict of the Tyrrell Sea.

211. See Lajeunesse and Allard, "The Nastapoka drift belt, eastern Hudson Bay: Implications of a stillstand of the Quebec-Labrador ice margin in the Tyrrell Sea at 8 ka BP," 65–76 (re: Tyrrell Sea); also, see Clark and Karrow, "Late Pleistocene water bodies in the St. Lawrence Lowland, New York, and regional correlations," 805–13 (re: Champlain Sea). The Champlain Sea also included parts of the present-day states of New York and Vermont.

212. Weisburd, "A Forest Grows in Antarctica," 40.

213. Weisburd, "A Forest Grows in Antarctica," 40–43.

which places them into the late Permian Period.[214] Even though it is typical for us to merely envision Antarctica as being a white desert of snow and ice, this reality of ancient forestation should not be surprising when we recall that the primeval landmass was once a part of the supercontinent of Gondwana, which, in Permian time, was much more florally plush, especially in its northern reaches.[215] While it has long been the predominant view of mainstream science that the Southern Continent has been fully and continuously glaciated for, at least, the last 35–40 million years—since the mid-Tertiary Period,[216] these discoveries of both very old and much more recent forests seem to show otherwise. Webb et al. have advocated for an Antarctic multi-glacial dynamic ice sheet model because they believe that geological evidences are strongly indicative of "one or more phases of deglaciation" within the last three million years.[217] In fact, it is their postulation that the most recent deglaciation—based on their studies (in addition to those of the fossil forests) of marine microfossils and glacial till on the east Antarctic ice sheet—occurred in the late Pliocene or early Pleistocene Epoch, probably *less than* three million years ago.[218] This general timeline is significant. In the greater context of deep time, this places a possible Antarctic deglacial event just a million years or less prior to the first known appearance of *Homo erectus* (viz., Adam; at 1.9 Ma—possibly even 2.0 Ma, per Wolpoff[219]), which is then sequentially followed, in our paradigm, by the Flood/Ice Age Event (near the old Pliocene-Pleistocene boundary at 1.81 Ma). In other words, at a somewhat recent point in Cenozoic time (3 Ma or earlier), there must have been a significant waning in the longstanding glaciation (which had existed

---

214. See Wamser, "UWM geologists uncover Antarctica's fossil forests."

215. Note that the Gondwanian forests were heavily inundated with the *Glossopteris* seed fern. Fossilized versions of these plants are abundant today in Antarctica. However, they became extinct at the End-Permian Event (c. 251 Ma) and thus are only found amidst the older forest sequences. This means that there are no *Glossopteris* fossils among the original remains of the younger forest (which consists of a different system of flora).

216. Ingolfsson, "Quaternary glacial and climate history of Antarctica," 3. Note that Ehrmann suggests 45.5 Ma.

217. Webb et al., "Late Neogene and older Cenozoic microfossils in high elevation deposits," 96. This concept of possible multi-deglaciations over time is especially interesting today in light of the recent concerns about the rapid melting of the Thwaites Glacier, nicknamed "The Doomsday Glacier," in West Antarctica. For more on this phenomenon, see Rignot et al., "Widespread, rapid grounding line retreat," 3502–9.

218. Webb et al., "Late Neogene and older Cenozoic microfossils in high elevation deposits," 96.

219. See Stallings, *The Genesis Column*, 116 (footnote). This makes reference to paleoanthropologist Milford Wolpoff.

since the mid-Tertiary Period, c. 35–40/45.5 Ma) in order for the youngest of the now fossil forests to first appear and to grow and flourish.[220] These factors all set the stage for the present day Antarctican glaciation—which, if Webb is correct, is actually a *re-glaciation*—to become initiated post-Flood.

The Ancient Plants that are Still Alive

There are currently living plants that have been determined to be notably antiquated. The existence of these plants is potential evidence for a Flood set further back in time than normally posited. Incidentally, the plants are also potential evidence in favor of an Old-Earth (at least, an Earth older than 6,000–10,000 years). There are two cases to be mentioned.

First, in the Jurupa Mountains of Riverside County, California, there is a Palmer's oak that is thought to be approximately 15,600 ± 2,500 years old.[221] This gives it a minimum age estimate of slightly in excess of 13,000 years (and a maximum age estimate of just over 18,000 years). Michael R. May et al. comments:

> We investigated a recently discovered disjunct population of Palmer's oak in the Jurupa Mountains of Riverside County, California. Patterns of allozyme polymorphism, morphological homogeneity, widespread fruit abortion, and evidence of fire resprouting all strongly support the hypothesis that the population is a single clone. The size of the clone and estimates of annual growth from multiple populations lead us to conclude that the clone is in excess of 13,000 years old. . . . The ancient age of the clone implies it originated during the Pleistocene and is a relict of a vanished vegetation community. Range contraction after climate change best explains the modern disjunct distribution of Q. palmeri [Palmer's oak] and perhaps other plants in California.[222]

This Pleistocene tree is now the oldest known living plant in the world. It has persevered through time by surviving the Ice Age, the current desert conditions, and numerous major forest fires.

---

220. Weisburd, "A Forest Grows in Antarctica," 40–43.

221. May et al., "A Pleistocene Clone of Palmer's Oak Persisting in Southern California," 1–11.

222. May et al., "A Pleistocene Clone of Palmer's Oak Persisting in Southern California," 1.

Second, there is a creosote bush in the Mojave Desert near Palm Springs, California that is thought to be approximately 11,700 years old.[223] This indicates that the bush clone originated in the late Pleistocene-early Holocene (in the immediate vicinity of the epochal boundary). The old creosote is the former oldest known living plant in the world.

If the age postulation of these olden plants is correct, then both had direct contact with the latest stage of the Quaternary Ice Age. The creosote bush experienced the final recession phase just prior to the Holocene Epoch and the Palmer's oak actually lived through anywhere from 1.3 to 3.9 thousand years of the final Pleistocene glacial encroachment. Also, since these plants are "a relict of a vanished vegetation community," the reasonable implication is that these extant relicts had ancestral predecessors. This means that the existence of these particular types of plants (and presumably others as well) is actually pushed back still earlier (probably much earlier) in post-Flood time. Therefore, within a global Flood model, we posit that these plants are significant for at least two reasons: [1] they are post-Flood (indicated by the fact that they exist),[224] which supports the idea that the Noahic Deluge occurred much earlier than the traditional YEC date of c. 4–4.5 ka; and [2] they are older than YEC models allow, which supports the idea that an Old-Earth paradigm is more accurate than a Young-Earth paradigm. Moreover, we would like to further suggest that the "vanished vegetation community" from which these extant relicts are derived, were likely part of the initial recovering plant profusion immediately following the Flood. It is fascinating that the proposed age of these plants fits very well with an understanding that the Noahic Flood occurred near the old Pliocene-Pleistocene boundary (1.81 Ma).

---

223. Vasek, "Creosote Bush: Long-Lived Clones in the Mojave Desert," 246–55.

224. The probable response from many OECs would be that the plants had nothing to do with the Flood, since—in a typical regional Flood view—the Deluge never touched California. We, however, disagree with the regional Flood view.

4

The Evidence of Tradition

> The heritage that we can now fully transmit is richer than ever before....
> The heritage rises, and man rises in proportion as he receives it. History
> is, above all else, the creation and recording of that heritage; progress is its
> increasing abundance, preservation, transmission, and use.[1]

Practitioners of the study of history have a truly challenging task: namely, to comprehend those ancient accounts, which in their original intervals have long since passed away, yet, through ardent transmission, have continued in some way to be preserved as tradition. In our human efforts to translate and understand these annals of long-ago, each successive generation is faced with the difficulty of having a mere wisp of moments with which to survey and decipher the recorded fragments of the ever increasingly inconceivable breadth and depth of eons. While many have come and gone before us and passed down through time what they have variously seen and known and received, those of us today need a sure referent by which to gauge the measure of its historical veracity and to try to put it all together. Apart from that, everything about tradition and heritage continues to have the appearance of being merely a jumbled and confusing heap of largely fractured and antiquated shards.

Thankfully, for us as Christians, we have that incontrovertible referent. The Great I AM—who is himself the provider and eyewitness of all history— is present and speaking with us. He has given to us his certain revelation (the

---

1. Durant and Durant, *The Lessons of History*, 101–2.

Scriptures) whereby both the peaks and the valleys of the ages can be sifted and sorted and appropriately framed. It is his pneumatic wisdom of eternity and the presence of his guiding Word that can provide the direction and the sure elucidation we require in order to believe.

It is in this light that we consider the supplemental evidence from human tradition. As we further seek to understand the Noahic cataclysm, in addition to the biblical revelation and any pertinent empirical trace evidence, there are many extra-biblical accounts of a mysterious and significant flood that occurred sometime in the antiquated past. According to Eric Lyons and Kyle Butt:

> Anthropologists who study legends and folktales from different geographical locations and cultures consistently have reported one particular group of legends that is common to practically every civilization. Legends have surfaced in hundreds of cultures throughout the world that tell of a huge, catastrophic flood that destroyed most of mankind, and that was survived by only a few individuals and animals. . . . Legends have been reported from nations such as China, Babylon, Mexico, Egypt, Sudan, Syria, Persia, India, Norway, Wales, Ireland, Indonesia, Romania, etc. . . . Although the vast number of such legends is surprising, the similarity between much of their content is equally amazing.[2]

James Perloff explains this amazing similarity: "In 95 percent of the more than 200 flood legends, the flood was worldwide; in 88 percent, a certain family was favored; in 70 percent, survival was by means of a boat; in 67 percent, animals were also saved; in 66 percent, the survivors had been forewarned; in 57 percent, they ended up on a mountain; in 35 percent, birds were sent out from the boat; and in 9 percent, exactly eight people were spared."[3]

These numbers alone represent something astounding. Yet, as always, there remain those who are skeptical as to what they mean. One common response of the skeptic is that a basal story may have been brought to various locations by the incursion of Christian missionaries, only to then become established or embellished over time. Another common response is that the large preponderance of these flood stories are simply the independent vestigial results of many local devastating floods that have occurred around the world throughout the many centuries.[4] As Francisco stated, "There is

---

2. Lyons and Butt, "Legends of the Flood," 102–3.
3. Perloff, *Tornado in a Junkyard*, 168.
4. One such skeptic is Frazer, who essentially denies a true Noahic connection to

The Evidence of Tradition

evidence for flooding in all parts of the earth, but these are not necessarily simultaneous."[5] Certainly, he is right; there have, of course, been many local floods throughout the world both before and since the Noahic Flood. That much is sure. And, no doubt, over time, many locales originated and developed their own legends and passed them on within their respective cultures. It is even quite possible that some of these local stories may have bled over into other adjacent societies. Frazer, who was not a global Flood advocate, takes it a step further and surmises that some of these "certainly fabulous" (i.e., in his meaning, "fabulous" = luxuriously and fallaciously enhanced) traditions may have even "been magnified into world-wide catastrophes."[6] Moreover, it is also indeed true that there are some local flood stories that simply and honestly relate the local experiences about past local floods without any intended global inference at all.[7]

Yet, is this the case for *all* (or even the preponderance) of those many stories across *all* of the continents? Here's the key question: Is the local story hypothesis the most satisfactory explanation for the vast body of extant stories which are so prevalent across the world and so similar? Or, is there another explanation that may be all the more reasonable? Again, we would do well to remember both the forest and the trees; as mentioned previously in another regard, we perhaps have become trained to see things quite often a bit too locally. Whether unwittingly or otherwise, localism can be a convenient way to disregard or completely miss the possibility of greater realities. We hold that it is much more plausible to believe that there are certain accounts of non-Noahic local events and there are also variant retellings of the

---

these traditions. He states: "[M]any of these resemblances are to be explained by simple transmission, with more or less of modification, from people to people, and many are to be explained as having originated independently through the similar action of the human mind in response to similar environment" (*The Great Flood*, 2–3). See also, Montgomery, *The Rocks Don't Lie*, 161–78.

5. Francisco, "Genesis," 139.

6. See Frazer, *The Great Flood*, 214–33. He speaks to this thought: "But though stories of such tremendous cataclysms are almost certainly fabulous, it is possible and indeed probable that under a mythical husk many of them may hide a kernel of truth; that is, they may contain reminiscences of inundations which really overtook particular districts, but which in passing through the medium of popular tradition have been magnified into world-wide catastrophes. The records of the past abound in instances of great floods which have spread havoc far and wide; and it would be strange indeed if the memory of some of them did not long persist among the descendants of the generation which experienced them" (217–18).

7. Please be aware that these particular stories have never had anything whatsoever to do with Noah and the biblical Flood. Sometimes local flood stories are truly just recollections of local floods.

The Genesis Cataclysm

singular Noahic global event. One does not cancel out the other. Keeping in mind the framework of Scripture, sheer logic surely dictates that there are both. Charles Martin reminds us of a very important truth. He states:

> Like the beginning of the universe, the reality of a global flood is in no way diminished by the various retellings of the story [or by the various legitimate accounts of local stories]. Just as innumerable creation myths tell us that there *must* have been a beginning, in whatever form, the flood myths around the world tell us that there *must* have been a flood.[8]

We strongly concur. It is not truly plausible to believe that such a degree of widespread similarity across continents, cultures, and time is merely coincidental or artificially derivative. Even Rad was impressed by the "distribution of the saga" with its "remarkable uniformity" throughout and believed that the local flood explanation was insufficient to account for the vast traditions.[9] According to Custance, though many of the flood stories are different in specific details with one another and with the biblical account (which, by the way, should be expected), there are elements inherent to virtually all of them: [1] the Flood's cause was due to the moral failure of humanity; [2] a forewarning of the impending Flood was given to one man; [3] the entire world was depopulated by the Flood catastrophe with a small seed of humanity preserved in order to repopulate; and [4] animals are a significant part of the stories.[10] Clark puts the matter in the greater perspective:

> [M]yths and legends have been preserved among almost all peoples on the earth. Although myths may not have any value as scientific proof, they are significant in indicating that some great event has left its impression in the minds of men. On the assumption that there was a flood such as the one described in the Bible, the evidence of legends among widely separated and primitive peoples is just what would be expected.[11]

We believe that the most probable explanation is that the origin of these many diverse and disparate, yet similar, flood stories is tied to the

---

8. Martin, *Flood Legends*, 24 (italics his).

9. Rad, *Genesis*, 124. He concludes that the Flood traditions as we have them "require the assumption of an actual cosmic experience and a primitive recollection which, to be sure, is often clouded and in part often brought to new life and revised only later by local floods."

10. Custance, "Flood Traditions of the World," 9–44.

11. Clark, *Genesis and Science*, 99.

The Evidence of Tradition

Babelian Dispersion, which was post-Flood.[12] *All* of the sprawling refugees of Babel were the descendant sons and daughters of Noah. They were still close enough to the actual Flood event to retain a strong residual memory. As the people groups (complete with their own unique languages) left the common community and migrated across the Earth, the ages passed and some of the details became distorted in the telling and re-telling of the Flood story. This is what Martin cleverly refers to as "telephone mythology."[13] The idea is similar to the old summer camp game when a large number of kids are placed in a big circle; a person whispers a message which is then passed on around the circle until it finally returns to the originator, usually with some notable degree of difference and embellishment. A similar process of transmission would occur after the Noahic Flood. Martin further explains:

> As time passes and those cultures begin to fragment into other cultures, we would expect to see other changes in the story; this is only natural. In fact, we would expect that the further from the source (both temporal and physical) the story moves, the more it would change. However, even more curiously, when we then add thousands of years, countless people, and a scattering of these people, we find that, despite changes, there are *still common threads*. The first view—the "local flood" or "independent evolution" view—can reasonably explain the differences in the versions. It cannot, however, explain all of the similarities. Indeed, how can we account for these common threads, unless we admit that the stories all originate from the same source? The telephone mythology view is the only view that explains both the similarities and the differences.[14]

Now, with that in mind, yet following our Old-Earth understanding, factor in the additional amplification of nearly two million years along with the expansive outward migration of further manifold populations. What is the most reasonable inference, then, about the widespread human traditions concerning a great Flood event? The best answer is really not that difficult to conceive. In fact, Lyons and Butt call it "obvious":

> What is the significance of the various flood legends? The answer seems obvious: (a) we have well over 200 flood legends that tell of a great flood; (b) many of the legends come from different ages and civilizations that could not possibly have copied any of the

---

12. For further about the Babelian Dispersion, see *The Genesis Column*, 130–32.
13. Martin, *Flood Legends*, 14.
14. Martin, *Flood Legends*, 15–16.

similar legends; (c) the legends were recorded long before any missionaries arrived to relate to them the Genesis account of Noah; and (d) almost all civilizations have some sort of flood legend. The conclusion to be drawn from such facts is that in the distant past, there was a colossal flood that forever affected the history of all civilizations.[15]

We concur with this thinking. Despite the glut of multitudinous and often diverse accounts, the Great I AM has indeed provided that sure referent which stands tall and true amidst the chaos. He has given to us his revelation which provides a framework of reality. That wider revelation includes the particular record of the worldwide Flood of Noah. These variant extra-biblical Flood traditions fit well, as they should, within that divine framework. It is through the scriptural revelation of God by which all of the broken and dispersed shards can become appropriately re-ordered and properly reassembled into the one truthful form.

In this light, all attempts to denigrate the significance of the widespread tradition of the Flood[16]—its *universal memory*—fall woefully short from a biblical-logical perspective. We believe that the best explanation for this "memory" is that its many variations are merely the lasting residuals (separated and isolated over time from the definitive preserved tradition and scriptural record and tainted by local embellishments and modifications[17]) of an event that could not be forgotten—one that has been passed down through the millennia—from generation to generation—by the descendants of Noah. John Urquhart provides this gripping insight:

> If this awful tragedy ever happened; if the entire human race perished save one family, and perished by the hand of God in

---

15. Lyons and Butt, "Legends of the Flood," 103.

16. For instance, see Enns, "How should we interpret the Genesis flood account?."

17. Note that it is a frequent claim that the earlier dating of the Babylonian flood narratives compared to the Genesis flood narratives (combined with certain story similarities between the two corpora) implies that the OT account must have used the *Epic of Atrahasis* and the *Epic of Gilgamesh* as sources. While this view is widespread, this is not an altogether logical deduction. If the Babylonian-Akkadian texts are older, it simply means that those accounts were written down first. It certainly does not mean that they are more accurate, that the Mosaic author used them as sources, or that the Chaldean tradition is the original. Moreover, it certainly does not mean that Israel derived the Flood idea from Babylon. Both Israel and the Church consider Genesis to be *divine revelation*. Additionally, it should not be forgotten that, according to the Scriptures, the Babylonians—and the Assyrians, Akkadians, Sumerians, Hittites, as well as the Medes, Scythians, Persians, Egyptians, etc.—are also descendants of Noah and thus could and should have their own disjunct version of the Flood story.

punishment of sin, then that judgment must have cast long shadows. Through generation after generation the story must have lived on. It must have been the most awful and solemn recollection of our race. Many things may have been forgotten, but that could not be forgotten.[18]

It seems that many people across the Earth over many centuries have indeed remembered "this awful tragedy" in their own unique manners. Yet, at the same time, there also seems to be an innate compulsion in many of us, as fallen creatures, to want to deny and forget that which just will not go away.

---

18. Urquhart, "The Testimony of Tradition to the Flood," 117.

5

The Final Thoughts

> It is the glory of God to conceal things,
> but the glory of kings is to search things out.[1]

The evidence of Scripture always carries the day. Scripture is both *a priori* and primary. All other evidences are secondary and—when properly interpreted—play a supportive role to the record of Scripture in the quest to understand reality. This is an important qualification, particularly when considering the veracity of the Noahic Flood. Since there is so much debate among researchers concerning the extant empirical Flood evidence, it is imperative that the scriptural message about the Flood be understood first and foremost. It is our unwavering assertion that the Genesis Flood text, along with the strong support of other biblical texts, provides powerful and convincing evidence for belief in a *global* Noahic Flood event.

---

1. Prov 25:2. In light of this OT proverb, remember the words of Paul as to the royal status of Christian believers in the present installment of the Kingdom of God, which anticipates the completed New Kingdom—"The saying is sure: If we have died with him, we shall also live with him; if we endure, we shall also reign with him" (2 Tim 2:11–12a; Rev 20:4–6; cf. 1 Pet 2:9). Those who live and reign with Christ (i.e., "kings") have and exercise full dominion; those with full dominion are faithful seekers of truth (i.e., those who "search things out"), none of which can be found without God's willful divulgence (Deut 29:29). Truth, among all other good things, is purely a gift from God (Jas 1:17), yet there is human co-participation in the Kingdom process. The giving of truth by God, as well as the seeking and finding of truth by his image-bearers, are glorious mutual Kingdom actions. Those seekers of truth who are also in Christ have the fullest access to the glory.

The Final Thoughts

Moreover, it is also our assertion that enough empirical trace evidence exists to provide *compelling* corroborative support to this claim. This is further reinforced by the vast flood traditions that pervade human cultures around the world. Yet, still, the most important qualification of all is that the special revelation of the Bible can indeed stand-alone if required—even if the human consensus interpretation of empirical data[2] seems to stand in total contradiction.[3] Of course, we do not think that to be the case here (we, in fact, believe that the composite empirical evidence for the Flood is powerfully cogent), although there will always be many who seek to provide explanations that challenge the ideas advocated by creationists and orthodox-evangelical Christians. Such challenges are not necessarily a bad thing. Challenges can sharpen our thinking. It is frequently the empirical research from those of differing perspectives and motivations that, plausibly *reinterpreted* within a scriptural framework, actually lend strength to the Christian worldview. This verily is often what happens. Remember, truth is always still truth, regardless of where it is found or who it is that finds it. The Source of truth is always ultimately God. The practice of evidential apologetics is a most honorable way to effectively explain and defend the hope from God that is in us (see 1 Pet 3:15). It can give substance to the witness of our faith.

For those who are interested in such things, there are many questions about the Flood that are still yet to be answered with certainty (e.g., matters concerning the Ark—its logistics, its final disposition, etc.; matters concerning the logistics of the animals—their arrival, care, dispersion, speciation, etc.). Many (perhaps most?) of them will probably never be answered in this life. However, while we believe these particular subjects to be of a more peripheral nature, for those who have an abiding interest in them (and in other similar sorts of matters), the divine dominion mandate must continue to be pursued. The scant presence of even an exact and narrow interest may well be the call of God upon an individual to follow that path of enquiry.

---

2. Remember, the fallenness of nature—including the marred human noetic dimension—can be blurring of its truth. This is why having the definitive scriptural parameters along with the guidance of the indwelling Holy Spirit are so important for the Christian researcher.

3. For instance, as a representative sample of this biblical contradiction view, note this statement by Frazer: "Now so far as the narratives speak of floods which covered the whole world [including, of course, even the biblical narrative], submerging even the highest mountains and drowning almost all men and animals, we may pronounce with some confidence that they are false; for, if the best accredited testimony of modern geology can be trusted, no such cataclysm has befallen the earth during the period of man's abode on it" (*The Great Flood*, 217).

In reality, for those with a scholarly devotion, all truth possibilities must continue to be earnestly explored. In so doing, humility must be exercised at a premium. The mere fact that we are always being compelled to seek more truth is itself attestation that there is always still more truth to be sought and discovered. Essentially, the more that we learn, the more that we realize just how little we know. The bottom of God's deep well remains always just out of our sight. Therefore, it is imperative that we always strive to stay humble as we carry out our investigative expeditions (see Matt 23:12[4]).

Along those lines, we must say that our dating of the Noahic Flood at two millennia or less before 1.81 Ma is an exercise in studied logical inference that is based upon our best comprehensive interpretation of gathered information. In this regard, our understanding (surely limited) is set forth in a paradigm designed to show a specific possibility for the time placement of a very definitive event. After all, we are certain that the Scriptures affirm—without question—that the Flood of Noah was both historical and global; therefore, it is an indisputable reality that the event as biblically presented had to occur at some point in chronological time. We surmise that the temporal juncture just prior to 1.81 Ma seems to be a reasonably plausible possibility. Having said that, however—if, at our entrance into the New Kingdom, the Great I AM were to say, "Well done, my good and faithful servant—you stood strong on my scriptural truth, but I've got to let you know that you did miss it just a bit on that time placement," our response, from bended knee and with bowed head, will simply be, "Yes, Lord." For when all is said and done, it really is much more about the *fact* of the Flood's occurrence as the Lord God authoritatively proclaims it than it is about the specific time range of its occurrence as we mere children of depravity venture to theorize it.

Still, we have been given dominion and the highest position in the created order. As such, God has given humanity a quest to seek and to understand the mysteries of this universe in which we have been placed. This quest is not merely given as an endeavor to find new information. Much more importantly, it is given as an endeavor to come to know in a greater way the Creator of all things—who is also the Truth in all things—and to develop a more formidable and ever deepening faith in that same One who made us and gave himself for us. In a word, our earnest seeking of truth enables us in the process to grow in the knowledge, grace, and love of God.

---

4. Matt 23:12—"[W]hoever exalts himself will be humbled, and whoever humbles himself will be exalted."

The Final Thoughts

THE CONCLUSION

It is our firm conviction that God has allowed the passage of time to cover the blatant earthen signs of the Noahic Flood in such a way, and just enough, as to require earnest seekers of truth to use their eyes of faith and their vision of the Kingdom meta-narrative—along with their empirical sight and senses—to view and interpret the richness of the evidence. Prerequisites in this quest include a great respect for the authority of Holy Scripture, a pure heart with a simple desire for God's truth, and a relentless willingness to look for both "the forest and the trees" (viz., to see the multitudes of seemingly unrelated small scenes always in light of the big picture). The negation of *any* of these necessities will completely nullify the veracity of one's conclusions. However, we strongly aver that the totality of these necessities can bring the historical truth of the mystery of the Noahic Flood into a much, much greater clarity.

Bibliography

Ager, Derek. *The Nature of the Stratigraphical Record*. Chicester, UK: John Wiley & Sons, 1993.
———. *The New Catastrophism*. Cambridge, UK: Cambridge University Press, 1993.
Aguirre, Emiliano and Giancarlo Pasini. "The Pliocene-Pleistocene Boundary." In *Episodes* 8(2) (June 1985) 116–20.
Aldinucci, Mauro, Massimiliano Ghinassi et al. "Climactic and tectonic signature in the fluvial infill of a late Pliocene valley." In *Journal of Sedimentary Research* 77(5) (May 2007) 398–414.
Anderson, Bernard W. "Genesis annotations." In *The New Oxford Annotated Bible*, edited by Herbert G. May and Bruce M. Metzger. New York, NY: Oxford University Press, 1973.
———. *Understanding the Old Testament*. Englewood Cliffs, NJ: Prentice Hall, 1986.
Archer, Gleason Jr. *A Survey of Old Testament Introduction*. Chicago, IL: Moody, 1964.
Austin, Stephen A., John R. Baumgardner et al. "Catastrophic Plate Tectonics: A Global Model of Earth History." Professional Paper. Pittsburgh, PA: Creation Science Fellowship, 1994.
———. "Did Landscapes Evolve?." Professional Paper. Dallas, TX: Institute for Creation Research, 1983. https://www.icr.org/article/211.
Balsiger, Dave and Charles E. Sellier, Jr. *In Search of Noah's Ark*. Los Angeles, CA: Sun Classic, 1976.
Barrick, William D. "Noah's Flood and it's Geological Implications." In *Coming to Grips with Genesis*, edited by Terry Mortenson and Thane H. Ury. 251–81. Green Forest, AR: Master, 2008.
Bates, Robert L. and Julia A. Jackson. *Dictionary of Geological Terms*. New York, NY: Anchor, 1984.
Baulig, Henry. "Peneplanes and Pediplains." In *GSA Bulletin* 68(7) (1957) 913–30.
Baumgardner, John R. "Numerical Simulation of the Large-Scale Tectonic Changes Accompanying the Flood." Professional Paper. Pittsburgh, PA: Creation Science Fellowship, 1986.
Bergeron, Louis. "Deep Waters." In *New Scientist* 155(2097) (August 30, 1997) 22–26.
———. "Stanford Study: Earth's early ocean cooled more than a billion years earlier than thought." In *Stanford News* (November 11, 2009). https://news.stanford.edu/news/2009/november9/ancient-sea-temperature-111109.html.
Bolfan-Casanova, N. "Water in the Earth's Mantle." In *Mineralogical Magazine* 69(3) (June 2005) 229–57.

BIBLIOGRAPHY

Brown, Francis, S. R. Driver et al. *The Brown-Driver-Briggs Hebrew and English Lexicon.* Peabody, MA: Hendrickson, 2006.

Brown, Walter T. *In the Beginning: Evidence for Creation and the Flood.* Phoenix, AZ: Center for Scientific Creation, 2008.

Browne, Malcolm W. "Whale Fossils High in Andes Show How Mountains Rose from Sea." In *The New York Times.* New York, NY: March 12, 1987.

Burnham, A. D. and A. J. Berry. "Formation of Hadean granites by melting of igneous crusts." In *Nature Geoscience* 10 (May 8, 2017) 457–61.

Calvo, Jose P., Maria V. Triantaphyllou et al. "Alternating diatomaceous and volcanistic deposits in Milo Island, Greece." In *Paleogeography, Paleoclimatology, Paleoecology* 321/322 (March 1, 2012) 24–40.

Chadwick, Arthur V. "Megabreccias: Evidence for Catastrophism." *Origins* 5(1) (1978) 39–46.

Chaffey, Tim and Jason Lisle. *Old-Earth Creationism on Trial.* Green Forest, AR: Master, 2008.

Chapman, Ben C. "The First Epistle of Peter." In *The Parallel Bible Commentary*, edited by Edward E. Hindson and Woodrow Michael Kroll, 2599–2617. Nashville, TN: Thomas Nelson, 1994.

Cita, Maria Bianca, Luca Capraro et al. "The Calabrian Stage redefined." In *Episodes* 31(4) (December 2008) 408–19.

Clark, David L. "The Arctic Ocean and Post-Jurassic Paleoclimatology." In *Climate in Earth History: Studies in Geophysics.* Washington D.C.: The National Academies, 1982.

Clark, Harold W. *Fossils, Flood, and Fire.* Escondido, CA: Outdoor Pictures, 1968.

———. *Genesis and Science.* Nashville, TN: Southern Publishing Association, 1967.

Clark, Peter and P. F. Karrow. "Late Pleistocene water bodies in the St. Lawrence Lowland, New York, and regional correlations." In *The Geological Society of America Bulletin* 95(7) (July 1984) 805–13.

Clarey, Tim L. "Local Catastrophes or Receding Floodwater? Global Geologic Data that refute a K-Pg (K-T) Flood/Post-Flood Boundary." In *Creation Research Quarterly* 54(2) (2017) 100–20.

Coffin, Harold G. "Famous Fossils from a Mountaintop." In *Origins* 1(1) (1974) 45–47.

Copan, Paul and William Lane Craig. *Creation out of Nothing.* Grand Rapids, MI: Baker, 2004.

Crowell, John C. "Continental Glaciation through Geologic Times." In *Climate in Earth History.* Reviewed by The National Research Council of the National Academy of Sciences. Washington D.C.: National Academy, 1980.

Custance, Arthur C. "Flood Traditions of the World." In *Symposium on Creation*, Vol IV, edited by Donald W. Patten. 9–44. Grand Rapids, MI: Baker, 1972.

Cvancara, Alan M. *A Field Manual for the Amateur Geologist.* San Francisco, CA: Jossey-Bass, 1995.

Davidson, Richard M. "Biblical Evidence for the Universality of the Genesis Flood." In *Creation, Catastrophe, and Calvary*, edited by John Templeton Baldwin. 79–92. Hagerstown, MD: Review and Herald, 2000.

———. "The Flood." In *Evangelical Dictionary of Biblical Theology*, edited by Walter A. Elwell. 261–63. Grand Rapids, MI: Baker, 1996.

———. "The Genesis Flood Narrative: Crucial Issues in the Current Debate." In *Andrews University Studies* 42(1) (2004) 49–77.

BIBLIOGRAPHY

Daley, Jason. "Nepalese Expedition Seeks to Find Out if an Earthquake Shrunk Mount Everest." In *Smithsonian Magazine* (April 15, 2019). https://www.smithsonianmag.com/smart-news/nepalese-expedition-wants-find-out-eathquake-shrunk-mount-everest-180971963/.

Davey, Melissa L. "Earth may have underground 'ocean' three times that on surface." In *The Guardian* (June 12, 2014). http://www.theguardian.com/science/2014/jun/13/earth-may-have-underground-ocean-three-times-that-on-surface.

Davis, Ellen F. and Richard B. Hays, editors. *The Art of Reading Scripture*. Grand Rapids, MI: Eerdmans, 2003.

de Leeuw, Nora H., C. Richard A. Catlow et al. "Where on Earth has our water come from?." In *Chemical Communications*, Advanced Article (October 2010).

Di Celma, Claudio, Gino Catalamessa et al. "Sedimentology, architecture, and sequence stratigraphy of course-grained, submarine canyon fills from Pleistocene (Gelasian-Calabrian) of the Peri-Adriatic Basin, Central Italy." In *Marine and Petroleum Geology* 27 (May 25, 2010) 1340–65.

Dillow, Joseph C. *The Waters Above*. Chicago, IL: Moody, 1981.

Dorsey, A. and A. Martin-Barajas. "Sedimentation and deformation in a Pliocene-Pleistocene transtentional supradetachment basin, Laguna Salada, north-west Mexico." In *Basin Research* 11 (1999) 205–21.

Doukhan, Jacques B. *The Genesis Creation Story: Its Literary Structure*. Berrien Springs, MI: Andrews University Press, 1978.

Durant, Will and Ariel. *The Lessons of History*. New York, NY: Simon and Schuster, 1968.

Enghof, Henrik. "Historical Biogeography of the Hoarctic: Area Relationships, Ancestral Areas, and Dispersal of Non-Marine Animals." In *Cladistics* 11(3) (September 1995) 223–63.

Enns, Peter. "How should we interpret the Genesis flood account?." In *BioLogos Forum*, 2011. http://biologos.org/questions/genesis-flood.

Ehrmann, Werner U. and Andreas Mackensen. "Sedimentological evidence for the formation of an East Antarctic ice sheet in Eocene/Oligocene time." In *Paleogeography, Paleoclimatology, Paleoecology* 93 (May 1992) 85–112.

Fenneman, Nevin M. *Physiography of Western United States*. New York, NY: McGraw-Hill, 1931.

———. *Physiography of Eastern United States*. New York, NY: McGraw-Hill, 1938.

Frakes, Lawrence A., Jane E. Francis et al. *Climate Modes of the Phanerozoic*. Cambridge, UK: Cambridge University Press, 1992.

Francisco, Clyde T. "Genesis." In *The Broadman Bible Commentary*, Vol. 1 (Revised), edited by Clifton J. Allen, 139–49. 12 volumes. Nashville, TN: Broadman, 1973.

Frazer, James G. *The Great Flood*. Albany, NY: Jason Colavito, 2013.

Fretheim, Terrence E. "Genesis." In *The New Interpreter's Bible*, Vol. 1, edited by Leander E. Keck, 398–402. 13 volumes. Nashville, TN: Abingdon, 1994.

Frye, John C. "Valley erosion since Pliocene 'algal limestone' deposition in Central Kansas." In *Kansas Geological Survey Bulletin* 60(3) (1945) 1–12.

Garner, Paul A. "Geology and the Flood." Leicester, UK.: The Genesis Agendum, 1997.

Gibbard, Philip L and Martin J. Head. "The Definition of the Quaternary System/Era and the Pleistocene Series/Epoch." In *Quaternaire* 20(2) (2009) 125–33.

Gibbard, Philip L., Martin J. Head et al. "Former Ratification of the Quaternary System/Period and the Pleistocene Series/Epoch with a base at 2.58 Ma." In *Journal of Quaternary Science* 25(2) (September 2009) 96–102.

BIBLIOGRAPHY

Gibbard, Philip L. and Martin Head. "The newly-ratified definition of the Quaternary System/Period and redefinition of the Pleistocene Series/Epoch, and comparison of proposals advanced prior to formal ratification." In *Episodes* 33(3) (September 2010) 152–58.

Gibbard, Philip L. and Thijs van Kolfschoten. "The Pleistocene and Holocene Epochs." In *A Geologic Time Scale*, edited by F. M. Gradstein, James G. Ogg et al, 442. Cambridge, UK: Cambridge University Press, 2004.

Gibbard, Philip L., Alan G. Smith et al. "What status for the Quaternary?." In *Boreas* 34 (2005) 1–6.

Green, Joel B. *Practicing Theological Interpretation*. Grand Rapids, MI: Baker, 2011.

———. *Seized by Truth*. Nashville, TN: Abingdon, 2007.

Green, Joel B. and David F. Watson, editors. *Wesley, Wesleyans, and Reading the Bible as Scripture*. Waco, TX: Baylor University Press, 2012.

Hampson, Gary. "Sediment Dispersal across Late Cretaceous Shelf, Western Interior Seaway, Northern Utah and Colorado, U.S.A." Professional Paper. London, UK: Imperial College—Department of Earth Science and Engineering, 2010.

Hanna, Martin F. "Science and Theology: Focusing the Complimentary Lights of Jesus, Scripture, and Nature." In *Creation, Catastrophe, and Calvary*, edited by John Templeton Baldwin. 172–208. Hagerstown, MD: Review and Herald, 2000.

Hasel, Gerhard F. "The Biblical View of the Extent of the Flood." In *Origins* 2(2) (1975) 77–95.

———. "The Fountains of the Great Deep." In *Origins* 1(1) (1974) 67–72.

Head, Martin J., Philip Gibbard et al. "The Tertiary: a proposal for its formal definition." In *Episodes* 31(2) (June 2008) 248–50.

Hill, Carol A. "The Noachian Flood: Universal or Local?." In *Perspectives on Science and Christian Faith* 54(3) (September 2002) 170–83.

Howell, J. V. "Epicontinental Sea." In *Glossary of Geology*. Washington D. C.: American Geological Institute, 1966.

Ingolfsson, Olafur. "Quaternary glacial and climate history of Antarctica." In *Extent and Chronology of Glaciation: South America, Asia, Africa, Australia, and Antarctica*, Vol. 3, edited by Jurgen Ehlers and Philip L. Gibbard. 3–43. Amsterdam: Elsevier Science, 2004.

Isaac, Mark. "Claim CC364: Marine Fossils on Mountains." In *Talk Origins Archive* (May 17, 2004). http://www.talkorigins.org/indexcc/cc364.html.

Izuka, Scott K and Johanna M. Resig. "Evidence of Late Pliocene-Early Pleistocene marine environments in the deep sub-surface of the Lihue Basin, Kauia, Hawaii." In *Palaios* 23(7) (July 2008) 442–51.

James, Noel P. and Yvonne Bone. "A Late Pliocene-Early Pleistocene, inner shelf, subtropical, seagrass-dominated carbonate: Roe Calcarenite, Great Australian Bight, Western Australia." In *Palaios* 22(4) (July 2007) 343–59.

Jeanloz, Raymond. "The Hidden Shore: Enough Water Could be Locked in the Earth to Fill the Oceans Ten Times Over." In *The Sciences* 33 (January-February 1993) 26–31.

Johnston, William Robert. "Facts and figures on sea level rise." Professional Paper. 1–3. April 2002. http://www.johnstonarchive.net/environment/sealevel.html.

———. "'What if all the ice melts?' Myths and Realities." Professional Paper. 1–9. December 2005. http://www.johnstonarchive.net/environment/waterworld.html.

Josephus. *Antiquities*. 1.1.3.

BIBLIOGRAPHY

Kaiser, Walter C, Jr. "The Literary Form of Genesis 1–11." In *New Perspectives on the Old Testament*, edited by J. Barton Payne. Dallas, TX: Word, 1970.

Kilibarda, Zoran and David B. Loope. "Jurassic aeolian oolite on a paleohigh in the Sundance Sea, Bighorn Basin, Wyoming." In *Sedimentology* 44: 391–404 (1997).

Kirschvink, Joseph L. "Late Proterozoic Low-Latitude Global Glaciation: the Snowball Earth." In *The Proterozoic Biosphere: A Multidisciplinary Study*, edited by J. William Schopf and Cornelis Klein, 51–52. Cambridge, UK: Cambridge University Press, 1992.

Kulp, J. Lawrence. "Deluge Geology." In *Journal of the American Scientific Affiliation* 2(1) (1950) 1–15.

Lajeunesse, Patrick and Michel Allard. "The Nastapoka drift belt, eastern Hudson Bay: Implications of a stillstand of the Quebec-Labrador ice margin in the Tyrrell Sea at 8 ka BP." In *Canadian Journal of Earth Science* 40 (2003) 65–76.

Lambert, David. *The Field Guide to Geology*. New York, NY: Checkmark, 2007.

Lawrence, Jesse F. and Michael E. Wysession. "Seismic Evidence for Subduction-Transported Water in the Lower Mantle." In *Earth's Deep Water Cycle*, edited by Steven D. Jacobsen and Suzan Van Der Lee. 251–61. Washington D.C.: American Geophysical Union (2006).

Lenton, Timothy M, Michael Crouch et al. "First plants cooled the Ordovician." In *Nature Geoscience* 5 (February 1, 2012) 86–89.

Longman III, Tremper and John H. Walton. *The Lost World of the Flood*. Downer's Grove, IL: InterVarsity, 2018.

Lyons, Eric and Kyle Butt. "Legends of the Flood." In *Reason & Revelation* 23(11) (2011) 102–3.

Macri, Patrizia, Fabio Speranza et al. "Magnetic Fabric of Plio-Pleistocene sediments from Crotone fore-arc basin." In *Journal of Geodynamics* 81 (November 2014) 67–79.

Maiorano, P., L. Capotondi et al. "Vrica-Crotone and Montalbano Jonico sections: A potential unit-stratotype of the Calabrian Stage." In *Episodes* 33(4) (December 2010) 218–33.

Martin, Charles. *Flood Legends: Global Clues of a Common Event*. Green Forest, AR: Master, 2009.

Martin, Edward N. "Empiricism." In *New Dictionary of Christian Apologetics*, edited by Gavin J. McGrath and W. C. Campbell-Jack. 231–33. Leichester, UK: Intervarsity, 2006.

May, Michael R., Mitchell C. Provance et al. "A Pleistocene Clone of Palmer's Oak Persisting in Southern California." In *PLoS One* 4(12)(e8346) (December 2009) 1–11. https://journals.plos.org/plosone/article?id=10.1371/journal.pone.0008346.

McDowell, Robert C. and Wayne L. Newell. "Quaternary System." Professional Paper. U.S. Geological Survey 1151-H. 2001. https://pubs.usgs.gov/pp/p1151/quat.html.

McGowran, Brian, Bill Berggren et al. "Neogene and Quaternary coexisting in the geological time scale: The inclusive compromise." In *Earth-Science Reviews* 96(4) (June 2009) 249–62. https://www.academia.edu/13651649/Neogene_and_Quaternary_coexisting_in_the_geological_time_scale_The_inclusive_compromise. Note that the on-line PDF edition is paginated as 1–14, which is the way we make reference in the footnotes.

McNamara, Ken. "Neogene." In *Prehistoric Life*, edited by Jill Hamilton. New York, NY: DK, 2009.

Montanez, Isabel P. and Christopher J. Poulsen. "The Late Paleozoic Ice Age: An Evolving Paradigm." In *Annual Review of Earth and Planetary Sciences* 41(1) (May 30, 2013) 629–56.

Montgomery, David R. *The Rocks Don't Lie*. New York, NY: W. W. Norton, 2012.

Montgomery, John Warrick. *Faith Founded on Fact*. Newburgh, IN: Trinity, 1978.

———. "Karl Barth and Contemporary Theology of History." In *Journal of the Evangelical Theology Society* 06(2) (Spring 1963) 39–49.

Morton, Glenn R. "The Demise and Fall of the Water Vapor Canopy: A Fallen Creationist Idea." Professional Paper. 2000. https://morton-yec-archive.blogspot.com/2016/04/the-demise-and-fall-of-water-vapor.html.

Moshier, Stephen. "Geology does not Support a Worldwide Flood." In *The Lost World of the Flood*, by Tremper Longman III and John H. Walton, 150–61. Downer's Grove, IL: InterVarsity Press, 2018.

Moshier, Stephen and Carol Hill. "Missing Time: Gaps in the Rock Record." In *The Grand Canyon—Monument to an Ancient Earth*, edited by Carol Hill et al., 99–107. Grand Rapids, MI: Kregel, 2016.

Mounce, William D. "Ancient." In *Complete Expository Dictionary of Old and New Testament Words*. 19–20. Grand Rapids, MI: Zondervan, 2006.

———. "Word." In *Complete Expository Dictionary of Old and New Testament Words*. 803 ("logos"). Grand Rapids, MI: Zondervan, 2006.

———. "World." In *Complete Expository Dictionary of Old and New Testament Words*. 808–9. Grand Rapids, MI: Zondervan, 2006.

Murck, Barbara. *Geology*. New York, NY: John Wiley & Sons, 2001.

Murikami, Motohiko, Kei Hirose et al. "Water in Earth's Lower Mantle." In *Science* 295(5561) (March 8, 2002) 1885–87.

Naish, Tim and Peter J. J. Kamp. "Pliocene-Pleistocene marine cyclothems, Wanganui Basin, New Zealand: a lithostratigraphic framework." In *New Zealand Journal of Geology and Geophysics* 38 (1995) 223–43.

Northrup, Bernard E. "The Geological Foundation Below the Noahic Flood Deposits" (February 1997). Professional Paper. http://www.1dolphin.org/belowflood.html.

Ogg, James G., Gabi Ogg et al. *Concise Geologic Timescale*. Cambridge, UK: Cambridge University Press, 2008.

Oard, Michael J. *An Ice Age Caused by the Genesis Flood*. El Cajon, CA: Institute for Creation Research, 1990.

Oard, Michael J. "A Post-Flood Ice-Age Model can Account for Quaternary Features." In *Origins* 17(1) (1990) 8–26.

Osgood, John. "The Date of Noah's Flood." In *Creation* 4(1) (March 1981) 10–13.

Patten, Donald Wesley. *The Biblical Flood and the Ice Epoch*. Grand Rapids, MI: Baker, 1966.

———. *Catastrophism and the Old Testament*. Seattle, WA: Pacific Meridian, 1988.

Payne, William P. "Foreward." In *The Genesis Column*, by W. Joseph Stallings. xi–xiv. Eugene, OR: Wipf and Stock, 2018.

Pearson, D. G., F. E. Brenker et al. "Hydrous mantle transition zone indicated by ringwoodite included within diamond." In *Nature* 507 (March 13, 2014) 221–24.

Perloff, James. *Tornado in a Junkyard: The Relentless Myth of Darwinism*. Arlington, MA: Refuge, 1999.

BIBLIOGRAPHY

Pervesler, Peter, Alfred Uchman et al. "Ichnological record of environmental changes in Early Quaternary (Gelasian-Calabrian) marine deposits of the Stirone Section, Northern Italy." In *Palaios* 26(9) (September 1, 2011) 578–93.

Plichta, Denise T. "Ancient Near Eastern Genealogies." In *Redemptive History & Theology*. https://redemptivehistorytheology.com/chapter-1-god-establishes-his-cosmic-temple-through-creation-gen-11-13-2/introduction-to-genesis-1/blog/chapter-4-the-generations-of-adam-gen-51-27/ancient-near-eastern-genealogies/.

Prosser, Giacomo, Mario Bentivenga et al. "Late Pliocene volcaniclastic products from Southern Apennines: distal witness of early explosive volcanism in the Tyrrhenian Sea." In *Geological Magazine* 145(4): 521–36 (July 2008).

von Rad, Gerhard. *Genesis*. Philadelphia, PA: Westminster, 1972.

Ramsey, Kelvin W. "Distribution of Late Pliocene and Quaternary Deposits in the Middle Atlantic Coastal Plain: Delaware, Maryland, and Virginia." In Geological Society of America *Abstracts with Programs* 33(2) (March 2001).

Rashi (Shlomo ben Yitzchak). *Bereishis*. Sapirstein Edition. Brooklyn, NY: Mesorah, 2019.

Richard, S. M., S. J. Reynolds et al. "Early Pleistocene to late Miocene basin deposits." Geologic mapping report. U.S. Geological Survey. 2009. https://mrdata.usgs.gov/geology/state/sgmc-unit.php?unit=AZQTs%3B0.

Richter, Sandra L. *The Epic of Eden*. Downer's Grove, IL: InterVarsity, 2008.

Rignot, E., J. Mouginot et al. "Widespread, rapid grounding line retreat of Pine Island, Thwaites, Smith, and Kohler glaciers, West Antarctica, from 1992 to 2011." In *Geophysical Research Letters* 41(10) (May 28, 2014) 3502–9. American Geophysical Union. http://10.1002/2014GL060140.

Roll, Gulnara, Natalia Alexeeva et al. "Aral Sea." Professional Paper. Burlington, VT: St. Michael's College—Lake Basin Management Initiative: Experience and Lessons Learned Brief, June 2003. https://www.worldlakes.org/uploads/aralsea_30sep04.pdf.

Ross, Hugh. *The Genesis Question*. Colorado Springs, CO: NavPress, 2001.

———. *A Matter of Days*. Colorado Springs, CO: NavPress, 2004.

Royer, Dana L., Robert A. Berner et al. "CO_2 as a primary driver of Phanerozoic climate." In *GSA Today* 14(3) (March 2004) 4–10.

Rupke, N. A. "Prolegomena to a Study of Cataclysmal Sedimentation." In *Why Not Creation?*, edited by Walter E. Lammerts, 152–57. Grand Rapids, MI: Baker, 1976.

Rush, David E. and Larry Vardiman. "Pre-Flood Vapor Canopy Radiative Temperature Profiles." Professional Paper. 1–11. El Cajon, CA: Institute for Creation Research, 1990. https://www.icr.org/i/pdf/technical/Pre-Flood-Vapor-Canopy-Radiative-Temperature-Profiles.pdf.

Ryan, William and Walter Pitman. *Noah's Flood: The New Scientific Discoveries about the Event that Changed History*. New York, NY: Touchstone-Simon and Schuster, 1998.

Sample, Ian. "Rough diamond hints at vast quantities of water inside the earth." In *The Guardian* (March 12, 2014). https://www.theguardian.com/science/2014/mar/12/rought-diamond-water-earth-wet-zone.

Sarfati, Jonathan. *Refuting Compromise*. Green Forest, AR: Master, 2004.

Scheiderich, K., A. L. Zerkle et al. "Molybdenum isotope, multiple sulfur isotope, and re-dox sensitive element behavior in early Pleistocene Mediterranean sapropels." In *Chemical Geology* 279(3–4) (December 13, 2010) 134–44.

Schulte, Peter, Laia Alegret et al. "The Chicxulub Asteroid Impact and Mass Extinction at the Cretaceous-Paleogene Boundary." In *Science* 327 (March 5, 2010) 1214–18.

Shea, William H. "The Antediluvians." In *Origins* 18(1) (1991) 10–26.

BIBLIOGRAPHY

Schultz, Gary. "Large Blob Discovered Deep in the Earth." In *SMU Newswise*. Dallas, TX: Southern Methodist University—Department of Geological Science (October 20, 1999).

Schmandt, Brandon, Steven D. Jacobsen et al. "Dehydration melting at the top of the lower mantle." In *Science* 344(6189) (June 13, 2014) 1265–68.

Shiga, David. "Ancient Earth was a barren water world." In *New Scientist* 201(2688) (December 30, 2008) 8.

———. "Earth may have had water from day one." In *New Scientist* 208(2785) (November 5, 2010) 12.

Smith, Alan G., Tiffany Barry et al. "GSSPs, global stratigraphy and correlation." In *Strata and Time: Probing the Gaps in our Understanding*, edited by D. G. Smith, R. J. Bailey et al., 37–68. Bath, UK: The Geological Society of London, 2015.

Smith, Denys B. "Rapid marine transgressions and regressions of the Upper Permian Zechstein Sea." In *Journal of the Geological Society* 136(2) (1979) 155–56.

Snelling, Andrew A. *Earth's Catastrophic Past*. Two vols. Dallas, TX: Institute for Creation Research, 2009.

Stallings, W. Joseph. *The Genesis Column*. Eugene, OR: Wipf and Stock, 2018.

Steinmann, Andrew E. "Gaps in the Genealogies in Genesis 5 and 11?" In *Bibliotheca Sacra* 174 (April-June 2017) 141–58.

Strong, James. *Hebrew and Aramaic Dictionary of the Old Testament*. Nashville, TN: Thomas Nelson, 1995.

Taylor, Paul F. *The Six Days of Genesis*. Green Forest, AR: Master, 2009.

Thompson, Alan Bruce. "Water in the Earth's Upper Mantle." In *Nature* 358(6384) (July 23, 1992) 295–302.

Tibuleac, Ileana Madalina and Eugene Herrin. "Lower Mantle Lateral Heterogeneity Beneath the Caribbean Sea." In *Science* 285(5434) (September 10, 1999) 1711–15.

Tyler, David J. "Flood Models and Trends in Creationist Thinking." In *Creation Matters* 2(3) (May/June 1997) 1–6.

Tyson, L. "A model for the Late Pliocene tectonics and its effects on Quaternary sedimentation in the Trinidad Area of the East Venezuelan Basin." Professional Paper. The Geological Society of Trinidad & Tobago. 2008. https://thegstt.org/geology/pliocene%20tectonics.htm.

Ullendorff, Edward. *Ethiopia and the Bible*. Oxford, UK: Oxford University Press, 2013. Originally published in 1968.

Unnamed author. "Cataclysm." In *Webster's New World Dictionary of the American Language*. Second Edition. New York, NY: William Collins & World, 1976.

Urquhart, John. "The Testimony of Tradition to the Flood." In *Bible League Quarterly* 152 (1937).

Vail, Isaac Newton. *The Earth Annular System*. London, UK: Ferris and Leach, 1912.

Vardiman, Larry. "Temperature Profiles for an Optimized Water Vapor Canopy." Professional Paper. San Diego, CA: Institute for Creation Research, 2013. http://www.icr.org/i/pdf/research/Canopy.pdf.

Vasek, Frank C. "Creosote Bush: Long-Lived Clones in the Mojave Desert." In *American Journal of Botany* 67(2) (1980) 246–55.

Veizer, Jan, Davin Ala et al. "87Sr/86Sr, δ13C and δ18O evolution of Phanerozoic seawater." In *Chemical Geology* 161 (1999) 59–88.

Velikovsky, Immanuel. *Earth in Upheaval*. New York, NY: Doubleday, 1955.

Webber, Robert E. *Who gets to Narrate the World?*. Downer's Grove, IL: IVP, 2008.

BIBLIOGRAPHY

Wesley, John. "The General Deliverance." In *The Works of John Wesley*, Vol. 2, edited by Albert C. Outler, 437–50. 35 vols. Nashville, TN: Abingdon, 1985.

———. "Witness of Our Own Spirit." In *The Works of John Wesley*, Vol. 1, edited by Albert C. Outler, 302–3. 35 vols. Nashville, TN: Abingdon, 1984.

Webb, Peter-Noel, David M. Harwood et al. "Late Neogene and older Cenozoic microfossils in high elevation deposits of the Transantarctic Mountains: Evidence for marine sedimentation and ice volume variation on the east Antarctic craton." In *Antarctic Journal* (1983 Review) 96–97.

Weisburd, Stefi. "A Forest Grows in Antarctica: An extensive forest may have flourished about 3 million years ago." In *Science News* 129 (March 8, 1986). https//www.thefreelibrary.com/A+forest+grows+in+Antarctica.-a04164401.

Whitcomb, John and Henry M. Morris. *The Genesis Flood*. Phillipsburg, NJ: P&R, 1961.

Wonderly, Dan. *God's Time-Records in Ancient Sediments*. Hatfield, PA: Interdisciplinary Biblical Research Institute, 1977.

Woods, Robert W. "How Old is the Earth?." In *Signs of the Times* 80 (April 1953) 8–15.

Woodmorappe, John. *Studies in Flood Geology*. El Cajon, CA: Institute for Creation Research, 1999.

Worsley, Thomas R. and Yvonne Herman. "Episodic Ice-Free Arctic Ocean in Pliocene and Pleistocene Time: Calcareous Nano-Fossil Evidence." *Science* 210(4467) (October 17, 1980) 323–25.

Ye, Yu, David A. Brown et al. "Compressibility and thermal expansion of hydrous ringwoodite with 2.5(3) wt% H2O." In *American Mineralogist* 97(4) (April 1, 2012) 573–82.

Young, Davis A. *The Biblical Flood*. Grand Rapids, MI: William B. Eerdmans, 1995.

———. *Creation and the Flood*. Grand Rapids, MI: Baker, 1977.

www.ingramcontent.com/pod-product-compliance
Lightning Source LLC
Chambersburg PA
CBHW050832160426
43192CB00010B/2002